Cookies

Cookies

MORE THAN 100 IRRESISTIBLE RECIPES

THUNDER BAY
P · R · E · S · S
San Diego, California

THUNDER BAY
P · R · E · S · S

Thunder Bay Press
An imprint of the Advantage Publishers Group
5880 Oberlin Drive, San Diego, CA 92121-4794
www.thunderbaybooks.com

Copyright © Salamander Books Ltd, 2003

A member of **Chrysalis** Books plc

All notations of errors or omissions should be addressed to
Thunder Bay Press, Editorial Department, at the above address. All other correspondence
(author inquiries, permissions) concerning the content of this book should be addressed to
Salamander Books Ltd, 8 Blenheim Court, Brewery Road, London, N7 9NY, U.K.

ISBN 1-57145-802-6
Library of Congress Cataloging-in-Publication Data available upon request.

Printed in China
1 2 3 4 5 07 06 05 04 03

CREDITS

PHOTOGRAPHERS: Neil Sutherland, Amanda Heywood, and Peter Barry EDITOR: Jillian Stewart
CONTRIBUTING EDITOR: Elizabeth Wolf-Cohen DESIGNER: Louise Clements PRODUCTION: Neil Randles,
Karen Staff COLOR SEPARATION: Anorax Imaging Limited, UK
PRINTED AND BOUND BY: Sino Publishing House Limited, China

THE AUTHOR

ELIZABETH WOLF-COHEN, who contributed the great majority of the recipes in *Cookies*, is a food writer, cook, and stylist with many years of experience. Liz lived and worked in France for four years, gaining her Grande Diplôme Culinaire before working in Parisian restaurants such as Dodin Bouffant and Maxims. She returned to New York to work at Lavin's Restaurant before moving to London, where she became a full-time cooking editor. Since 1985, Liz has been a freelance cooking writer and stylist, contributing to *Taste* and *Australian Vogue Entertaining* magazines. A member of the Guild of Food Writers, she has also written a variety of cookbooks, including *The Chocolate Cookbook*, *The New Jewish Cuisine*, and *The French Recipe Cookbook*.

PUBLISHER'S NOTE

The artifacts and advertisements featured in this title are for illustration purposes only; none of the organizations whose artifacts or advertisements are featured have been involved in any way in creating the recipes that appear in this book, and the publishers wish to state that the use of particular artifacts or advertisements with specific recipes is in no way intended to imply that the recipe in question has been supplied, created, or approved by the particular organization.

Contents

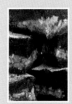
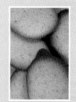

Introduction

Cookies: The word alone is enough to conjure up enticing images of plates piled high with rich chocolate and nut indulgences. Derived from the Dutch *koekje*, meaning "little cake," the cookie came to North America with the first ships to New Amsterdam, and as far as the rest of the world is concerned, it never went home. Cookies are as American as apple pie and yet, in just the same way, they are found the world over, in almost every cuisine.

The Germans and Austrians bake some of the best cookies of all, redolent with ginger and anise, poppy seeds and nutmeg, and occasionally coated with dark, luscious chocolate. These were famous as Christmas treats, and they have been made since medieval times, when merchants traveled to the very farthest reaches of the known world to bring back rare spices.

But England became the heartland of the cookie in the nineteenth century with

relatively plain and delicately flavored cakes, baked to a particularly crisp texture. The biscuit, as cookies are known in England, became the natural partner for a cup of English tea and, since 1870, it has been sold in hundreds of varieties and shapes. At Christmastime, English biscuits are still sold as valued gifts in cheerfully decorated, airtight tins that keep the contents crisp throughout the holidays.

Many other countries have strong traditions of making and baking little cakes.

The Chinese, for instance, have two or three favorite flat wafers, which are cut in rectangles or squares, plain or sandwiched with bean paste, or twisted to hold a little good luck sign, which have now been adapted in America as fortune cookies.

Spanish and Portuguese bakers turn out platters of tiny delicacies for a late breakfast and for afternoon coffee; little tarts of lemon curd and honey, tiny filled cookies with coffee cream or praline icing, and pinwheel slices of vanilla and orange.

And finally, the American cookie—its name from the Dutch, its texture more cakey than its English cousins, its strong flavors with a heavy emphasis on chocolate and various nuts, and its chewy, satisfying mouthful.

We have borrowed recipes from the world that are now uniquely American. There are cookies made in every region and every state, almost in every town and city. A Chicago cookbook from the 1920s offers 365 cookie recipes, one for every day of the year, and claims it could have provided as many again.

So explore the great heritage of cookies, with old-fashioned favorites and newly imagined delicacies. New and unusual recipes will add delicious (and fast-disappearing) variety to the contents of your cookie jar, so go ahead and experiment. And while you're enjoying those wonderful cookies, marvel at the fascinating variety of cookie jars that are now so coveted by collectors.

Producing Perfect Cookies

There is no secret to achieving perfect results—just follow these simple guidelines.

Ingredients

Most cookies are made from a dough paste of butter, sugar, eggs, and flour in varying proportions. Because the true flavors of the ingredients really come through in cookies, it is important to use the best ingredients.

Flour and Grains

All-purpose flour is a blend of hard and soft wheats. Unbleached flour is preferred by many cooks because it is more natural and contains more vitamins, but both give equally good results. Whole-wheat flour contains the wheat germ and is heavier than all-purpose. Using all whole-wheat flour is fine if you want a high-fiber cookie, otherwise combine it with white flour for better results.

Oats are often added to cookies to enhance flavor, texture, fiber, and nutrients. Old-fashioned rolled oats and quick-cooking oats (not instant oats) are best for baking.

Chemical Raising Agents

Baking soda combines with other acid ingredients such as sour cream, lemon juice, or honey to raise the dough. This action begins almost immediately, so any doughs containing baking soda should be baked as soon as they are mixed. Baking powder is a combination of baking soda and an acid salt, usually cream of tartar. Most baking powders provide two raising actions: the first when it comes into contact with the liquid

ingredients, the second when the dough is heated. For this reason, the doughs should be mixed and baked immediately. Cream of tartar is used when beating egg whites for meringues and some icings to add stability.

Sugars and Sweeteners

Granulated sugar is the most commonly used sugar. However, it can show up as brown flecks in more delicate cookies. Superfine sugar is ideal for baking tender cookies, since it dissolves and creams easily. Confectioners' sugar is made by grinding granulated sugar and adding a little cornstarch in order to prevent caking. Light and dark brown sugar—granulated sugar with molasses added—add a dense, chewy texture to cookies.

Unsulfured molasses is a syrup made from boiled cane or beet sugar dissolved in water during the initial refining process. Black strap molasses is the very dark, strong residue from the third boiling. Maple syrup has a deep golden color and distinctive flavor.

Use 100 percent real maple syrup for flavoring cookies. Corn syrup tends to absorb moisture, so is useful for keeping baked goods moist. Honey, either runny or set, provides moisture and texture in cookies.

Eggs and Dairy Products

Eggs provide texture, structure, flavor, and moisture to cookies. Unless specified, use large eggs in the recipes. Pregnant women, babies, and the elderly should avoid eating raw or undercooked eggs and meringues.

Unsalted butter is preferable for all baking. Since it contains no salt, which acts as a preservative, it tends to be fresher than salted butter and also contains slightly less water and other impurities.

Cream and milk come in many forms, usually according to their butterfat content. Unless specified in the recipes, use whole milk, or sour cream (about 18 percent fat) and plain yogurt, as skim or low-fat versions may not provide enough fat.

Chocolate and Cocoa

Unsweetened chocolate is very dry and bitter, but has an intense chocolate flavor ideal for cookies and brownies. Semisweet chocolate contains more sugar than bittersweet; the latter gives a more intense chocolate flavor to most recipes. In the U.S., dark chocolate must contain 34 percent solids, but the best results are obtained with chocolate containing a minimum of 50 percent cocoa solids. Milk chocolate has a lower cocoa solids content and cannot be substituted for dark, bittersweet, or semisweet chocolate.

Chocolate chips are designed to keep their shape when baked, although they can be melted. When buying a white chocolate, choose a high-quality brand (such as confectionery coating). As with milk chocolate, it should be melted with care. When buying cocoa, look for Dutch-processed cocoa powder, which has a reddish color and milder flavor than the more common varieties.

Fruits and Nuts

Dried fruits add flavor and texture to many cookies. Raisins, golden raisins, and currants are often used, but the range of dried fruits available is rapidly expanding. Try dried cranberries, sour cherries, blueberries, figs, apples, pears, and mango. Nuts almost always benefit from a light toasting to bring out their flavor, so if you have the time, try doing this before adding them to the mixture.

Flavorings

Spices are found in almost every cookie. Cinnamon, nutmeg, and ginger are common, but you can also try cloves, mace, crushed cardamom seeds, and allspice. Grinding your own spices adds a more intense flavor—try using a clean coffee grinder. Vanilla extract is the most convenient form of vanilla, but always use a pure extract. Vanilla beans are expensive but give wonderful results. Split a vanilla bean lengthwise with a sharp knife and scrape out the tiny black seeds.

Equipment

Most cookies can be made using the basic equipment found in any ordinary kitchen. However, be sure to read the recipe thoroughly before you start, so that you can be certain of having all the necessary equipment, as well as all the required ingredients.

Measuring spoons and cups are essential for all home baking. Be sure to use measuring spoons and cups, not ordinary kitchen spoons and cups, for reliable results.

Heatproof glass measuring cups should be used to measure liquids.

Most cookies can be made by hand—after all, they were all made that way at first—but using an electric mixer, either a heavy-duty counter model or a handheld type, saves both time and energy. For most cookies, a handheld mixer is ideal, as it gives a feel of control over the dough. Some cookie doughs can be made with a food processor, although it is mostly used for chopping other ingredients such as nuts and chocolate, for which they are simply indispensable.

Other general kitchenware useful in cookie-making are good mixing bowls, sturdy wooden spoons for beating and creaming, and rubber spatulas and plastic dough scrapers for scraping out bowls and work surfaces. A selection of whisks and good knives is also essential. A pastry wheel is handy for cutting various cookies. A double boiler can be

useful, although a mixing bowl set over a saucepan makes a perfect substitute.

A rolling pin is essential for rolling out cookie doughs quickly and evenly. Many styles are available, some with handles and some without. Particularly good are the Teflon varieties, which really do not stick (not often, anyway!). A long ruler is essential for measuring, and the straight edge is useful as a cutting guide.

Small ice cream scoops are ideal for forming drop cookies, and guarantee uniformly sized cookies. Cookie cutters of all sizes and shapes are available. Look for unusual ones in party stores and mail-order catalogs. Everything from lovable animals and cartoon characters to the more traditional gingerbread children are available, and there are many more for any occasion!

A cookie press or cookie gun is essential for "spritz" (see page 232) and other molded cookies. They come with a variety of disks used to make different shapes. Other special molds, such as those used for making shortbread or "springerle," are available at specialty shops or by mail order.

When baking cookies, use heavy-gauge, flat, shiny aluminum baking sheets, which should be at least 2 inches smaller than the inside of your oven so that the heat can circulate evenly. Dark cookie sheets can absorb too much heat and cause the bottoms of the cookies to burn or cook too quickly. Very thin baking sheets may warp, distorting the shape of the cookies.

Nonstick sheets are ideal for certain cookies, but may cause others to spread too much, so follow the instructions for each recipe. New cushionaire baking sheets with

an insulated base are excellent, especially for thin cookies or meringues, which can stick or overbrown on the bottom.

Other pans useful for making bar cookies, brownies, and shortbread are a 9-inch jelly-roll pan, a 13 x 9-inch baking pan, a 15½ x 10½-inch jelly-roll pan, and 8- or 9-inch cake and tart pans, preferably with removable bottoms. If using a Pyrex baking dish, reduce the oven temperature by 25°F. Wire cooling racks, pancake turners, and various metal palette knives are essential for cooking and removing cookies quickly and neatly from their baking sheets.

Pastry or decorating bags with a selection of tips can be used to pipe meringues and soft cookie doughs, as well as various kinds of icings.

Papers, foils, and plastics are really useful for cookie-making. Nonstick baking parchment is ideal for most jobs—although more expensive than other baking papers, it is well worth the extra cost. This special silicone-coated, greaseproof paper can withstand direct contact with oven heat, so, unlike waxed paper, it will not burn. It is ideal for lining baking sheets for sticky cookies and meringues, lining cake pans, and making paper cones (see recipe for Cream Cheese Macadamia Nuts, page 81). Waxed paper, a paraffin-coated tissue paper, is inexpensive and particularly good for wrapping doughs that need to be refrigerated.

Colored cellophane is useful for transforming little bags of goodies into attractive gifts with a happy sparkle. Plastic wrap is a lifesaver, ideal for wrapping and covering doughs and icings, it can also be used to help roll out sticky doughs. Aluminum foil is good for lining baking sheets and can make cleanup much easier. Another useful product is a Teflon-coated material increasingly used by professionals, which creates a completely nonstick surface. It is available in sheets that can be cut to fit baking sheets, pans, and griddles. Once used, it can simply be wiped clean and used again. Look for it in specialty shops and mail-order catalogs.

Techniques & Tips

It is essential to master certain techniques for cookie-making. Most cookie doughs start by creaming the butter and sugar, then adding the liquid and dry ingredients. For the best results, all the ingredients should be at room temperature.

To cream the butter and sugar, use an electric mixer at a low speed. Increase the speed to medium and beat until the mixture lightens in color and texture and looks light and fluffy; this takes about two minutes. Alternatively, beat the butter first to soften it, then add the sugar and beat until it becomes light and fluffy.

To beat whole eggs or yolks, usually with sugar, use an electric mixer at low speed to combine until blended, then increase the speed to medium and beat until the eggs are thickened and lightened in texture, about two to five minutes depending on the recipe.

To beat egg whites, be sure all the equipment is clean and free of grease. Use an electric mixer at low speed and beat until the whites are frothy. Add the cream of tartar or salt, if the recipe directs, and increase the speed to medium-high until soft peaks form. For stiff peaks, beat a little longer until sharp peaks form when the beater is lifted out. If adding sugar for meringues, it should be added gradually once the soft peaks form.

To fold in beaten egg whites or other

For Delicious Cookies Everybody Likes.

Standard Sugar Cookies

for recipe see page 33

ingredients without deflating a mixture, use a large metal kitchen spoon or rubber spatula to gently cut down through the center and along the side of the bowl in a circular movement, to combine the mixtures while losing as little air as possible.

To melt chocolate, chop it and put it in the top of a double boiler set over the bottom pan of barely simmering water. Stir until melted and smooth. Alternatively, put the chocolate in a heatproof bowl set over a saucepan of barely simmering water. It is essential that no liquid comes into contact with the chocolate, since it may cause it to seize and harden. Chocolate can be melted in the microwave, but be careful not to overheat and burn it. Microwave four ounces of chopped dark chocolate on medium power (50 percent) for about two minutes, then remove and stir until smooth. Decrease the power to low (30 percent) for milk and white chocolate. If not completely melted, microwave for five to ten seconds at a time until completely melted and smooth.

To grind nuts finely, use a food processor fitted with a metal blade, using the pulse action until fine crumbs form. If the recipe includes sugar or flour, add a tablespoon of either with the nuts to keep them from being overprocessed.

Top Tips for Perfect Results

● BEFORE YOU START, read the recipe and assemble everything you will need. Be sure the ingredients are at room temperature (unless otherwise stated)—adding cold eggs to a butter mixture can cause it to curdle.

● MEASURE AND SIFT together the dry ingredients before starting. This ensures that any spices and leaveners are well blended and the mixture is well aerated.

● MEASURE LEAVENERS by a level, not heaping, measuring spoon, and liquids in a glass measuring cup at eye level.

● STIR IN any small, chopped ingredients by hand so that they are evenly distributed.

● EGGS should be beaten lightly before being gradually added to a creamed butter-sugar mixture, to avoid curdling. If the mixture does curdle, stir in a tablespoon of the

measured dry ingredients, then continue with the recipe.

● MOST BUTTER-RICH COOKIE DOUGHS don't require greased baking sheets, but a thin layer of vegetable shortening (butter can burn) can be used as a precaution. For the lightest coating, use an oil spray. Otherwise, use a pastry brush for a light, even coating of oil, or line with foil or nonstick baking parchment.

● BE SURE the oven is preheated to the temperature required.

● ARRANGE COOKIES evenly on baking sheets, trying not to leave any large, empty areas. Leave enough room for cookies to spread. Chilling the dough before arranging on baking sheets helps prevent spreading.

● TRY TO BAKE COOKIES one sheet at a time in the center of the oven so that the air circulates evenly. Otherwise, rotate the baking sheets from the bottom shelf to the top shelf and from back to front halfway through the cooking time.

● NEVER USE a hot baking sheet. For quick cooling, run the back of the baking sheet under cold water, wipe dry, and regrease. Alternatively, arrange cookies on sheets of foil or baking parchment cut to fit the baking sheets. As soon as baked cookies are removed from the baking sheet, slide a prepared sheet of foil or parchment onto the baking sheet and bake immediately.

● BAKING TIMES CAN VARY. Begin by testing at the minimum time. Because they are relatively thin, cookies continue to bake after they are removed from the oven. Allow them to firm slightly before removing from the baking sheet. Let the cookies cool completely in a single layer on a wire rack before storing.

● STORE most cookies in airtight containers or tins. Store different kinds separately, since the flavors might blend, or moist cookies might soften crisp ones. Separate delicate or sticky cookies with waxed paper or foil. To recrisp, reheat for three to five minutes on a baking sheet in a 300°F oven.

● REFRIGERATOR COOKIE DOUGH can be made ahead and then frozen. Thaw in the refrigerator until just soft enough to slice.

Drop
cookies

Applesauce Spice Cookies

These soft, tender cookies have a mellow, spicy flavor.
If you don't like nuts, substitute some chopped dates or raisins.

Makes about 3 dozen cookies

1/2 cup (1 stick)
  butter, softened

1/2 cup packed light
  brown sugar

1/3 cup sugar

1 egg

1 teaspoon vanilla
  extract

1 cup applesauce

2 cups all-purpose flour

1 teaspoon baking soda

1/2 teaspoon salt

1 teaspoon ground
  cinnamon

1 teaspoon ground ginger

1/2 teaspoon ground
  cloves

1 cup golden raisins

3/4 cup chopped walnuts
  or pecans

 *Drop Cookies*

1. Preheat the oven to 350°F. Lightly grease two large baking sheets. In a large bowl, using an electric mixer, beat the butter for about 1 minute, until creamy. Add the sugars and beat the mixture for 1–2 minutes, until light and fluffy. Beat in the egg and vanilla extract, then stir in the applesauce.

2. In a medium bowl, stir together the flour, baking soda, salt, and spices. Stir into the butter-sugar mixture until well blended, then stir in the raisins and walnuts or pecans.

3. Drop tablespoonfuls of the mixture about 1½ inches apart onto the baking sheets. Bake for 5–7 minutes, until golden. Remove the baking sheets to wire racks to cool for 2–3 minutes. Move the cookies to wire racks to cool completely. Repeat with theremaining mixture. Store in an airtight container.

RIGHT: *The 1933 movie* King Kong *influenced the design of these cookie jars!*

Death by Chocolate

These cookies are large and flat, crisp on the edge, soft in the center, and filled with chocolate. **Makes about 2 dozen large cookies**

Vegetable oil spray
or vegetable oil,
for greasing

9 oz. bittersweet or
semisweet chocolate,
chopped

3/4 cup (1 1/2 sticks)
unsalted butter,
cut into pieces

3 eggs

3/4 cup superfine sugar

1/3 cup packed brown
sugar

2 teaspoons vanilla
extract

1/2 cup all-purpose
flour

6 tablespoons cocoa
powder, sifted

1 1/2 teaspoons baking
powder

1/4 teaspoon salt

9 oz. semisweet
chocolate, chopped
into 1/4-inch pieces,
or 1 1/2 cups semisweet
chocolate chips

6 oz. chocolate,
chopped into
1/4-inch pieces

6 oz. white
chocolate, chopped
into 1/4-inch pieces

1 1/2 cups pecans
or walnuts,
toasted and
chopped

1. Preheat the oven to 325°F. Lightly spray or grease two large baking sheets. In a medium saucepan over low heat, melt the chocolate and butter, stirring frequently until smooth. Set aside to cool slightly.

2. In a large bowl, using an electric mixer, beat the eggs and sugars for 2–3 minutes on low speed, until thick and pale. Gradually beat in the melted chocolate and vanilla extract until well blended. In a small bowl, stir together the flour, cocoa powder, baking powder, and salt until blended, then gently stir into chocolate mixture. Stir in the chocolate pieces and nuts.

3. Drop heaping tablespoonfuls of the mixture at least 4 inches apart onto the baking sheets. Wet the bottom of a drinking glass and use to flatten each dough ball slightly, to make each about 3 inches in diameter; you will only fit 4–6 cookies on each sheet. Bake for 10 minutes, until the tops are cracked and shiny. Do not overbake the cookies or they will break when you try to remove them from the baking sheet.

4. Remove the baking sheets to wire racks to cool slightly and set. Using a thin-bladed metal spatula, carefully move each cookie to wire racks to cool completely. Repeat with the remaining dough. Store in an airtight container.

Brown Sugar Cookies

This stiff dough bakes to a crisp, golden brown cookie that is perfect served on its own or as an accompaniment to ice cream. **Makes about 3 dozen cookies**

Vegetable oil spray
  or vegetable oil,
  for greasing
1¼ cups packed light
  brown sugar
3 tablespoons corn
  syrup
4 tablespoons water
1 egg
2⅓ cups all-purpose
  flour

1 tablespoon ground
  ginger
1 tablespoon baking
  soda
¼ teaspoon salt
1 cup finely
  chopped pecans

1. Preheat the oven to 375°F. Lightly spray or grease two large baking sheets. In a large bowl, using an electric mixer, beat the brown sugar, corn syrup, water, and egg until light.

2. Sift the flour, ginger, baking soda, and salt into a bowl and stir into the brown sugar mixture. Add the pecans and stir until well blended.

3. Drop heaping teaspoonfuls of the

mixture 2 inches apart onto the baking sheets. Bake for 10–12 minutes, until lightly browned. Remove the baking sheets to wire racks to cool slightly. Using a thin-bladed metal spatula, move the cookies to wire racks to cool. Repeat with the remaining mixture. Store in an airtight container.

RIGHT: *Cookie jars in the shape of clocks are common, but this is a particularly good example.*

Chocolate Turtles

This old-time favorite is enriched with extra chocolate and nuts. The pecans are meant to resemble the head, arms, and legs of a turtle. **Makes about 2 dozen cookies**

12 oz. semisweet chocolate, chopped

3 oz. unsweetened chocolate, chopped

1/4 cup (1/2 stick) unsalted butter, cut into pieces

1 1/2 cups sugar

4 eggs, lightly beaten

1 teaspoon vanilla extract

1/2 cup all-purpose flour

1 tablespoon instant espresso powder

1/2 teaspoon baking powder

1/4 teaspoon salt

2 cups coarsely chopped pecans

2 cups semisweet chocolate chips

2 cups pecan halves, for decorating

1. Preheat the oven to 350°F. Line two large baking sheets with foil or nonstick baking parchment. In a medium saucepan over medium-low heat, melt the chocolates with the butter until smooth, stirring frequently.

2. Add half the sugar and continue stirring until dissolved. Remove the pan from the heat and beat in the eggs, remaining sugar, and vanilla extract.

3. Sift together the flour, espresso powder, baking powder, and salt into a medium bowl. Stir into the chocolate mixture until blended, then stir in the chopped nuts and chocolate chips.

4. Using an ice cream scoop or ¼-cup measure, drop dough onto the baking sheets at least 3 inches apart and flatten slightly. Insert five pecans into the edge of each cookie to represent the head and legs of a turtle. Bake, one sheet at a time, in the center of the oven for about 10 minutes, just until the surfaces of the cookies begin to split. Do not overbake; the cookies should be soft in the center.

5. Remove the baking sheets to wire racks to cool slightly. Gently peel off the foil or paper and cool completely. Repeat with the remaining cookie dough and nuts. Store in an airtight container.

Raisin 'n' Lemon Cookies

These crumbly, melt-in-the-mouth cookies have a delicate lemon flavor and are ideal as an afternoon snack.

Makes about 18 cookies

Vegetable oil spray
or vegetable oil,
for greasing
1/2 cup (1 stick)
unsalted butter,
softened
1/2 cup sugar
Finely grated zest
of 1 lemon
1 egg, beaten

1 1/2 cups all-purpose
flour
2 teaspoons baking
powder
Pinch of salt
4 tablespoons
quick-cooking
oats
1 cup raisins

1. Preheat the oven to 375°F. Lightly spray or grease two large baking sheets. In a large bowl, beat the butter, sugar, and lemon zest together until thick and pale. Gradually beat in the egg until blended.

2. Sift the flour, baking powder, and salt into a bowl and stir into the butter mixture, with the oats, until blended. Stir in the raisins until just blended.

3. Drop heaping teaspoonfuls of the mixture at least 3 inches apart onto the baking sheets and flatten slightly with the back of a fork. Bake for 15–20 minutes, until golden brown. Remove the baking sheets to wire racks to cool for 2–3 minutes; transfer the cookies to wire racks to cool completely. Repeat with the remaining mixture. Store in an airtight container.

LEFT: *Bud and Jack
cookie jars, made
by the Robinson-
Ransbottom Pottery,
Roseville, Ohio.*

CLOCKWISE FROM RIGHT: *Chocolate Nut Crackles, Lacy Oatmeal Wafers, and Coconut Macaroons*

Chocolate Nut Crackles

These chocolate-coffee-nut cookies are big, rich, and intensely flavored.
Do not overbake or they will be dry. **Makes about 20 cookies**

9 oz. bittersweet or
  semisweet chocolate
3 oz. unsweetened
  chocolate, chopped
½ cup (1 stick) plus
  1 tablespoon butter,
  softened
6 tablespoons
  all-purpose flour
½ teaspoon baking
  powder

3 eggs
1 cup sugar
1 tablespoon instant
  espresso powder
1 tablespoon vanilla
  extract
1½ cups pecans,
  coarsely chopped
1½ cups hazelnuts,
  coarsely chopped

1½ cups semisweet
  chocolate chips

1. In a medium saucepan over low heat, melt the chocolates with the butter until smooth, stirring frequently. Set aside to cool. Sift the flour and baking powder into a small bowl and set aside.

2. Preheat the oven to 325°F. In a large bowl, using an electric mixer, beat the eggs with the sugar for about 2 minutes, until light and fluffy. Beat in the melted chocolate mixture, then the espresso powder and vanilla extract, until well blended. Add the flour mixture and beat until just combined, then stir in the nuts and chocolate chips.

3. Using a ½-cup measure, scoop out the cookie dough and arrange in mounds at least 3 inches apart on large, ungreased baking sheets. Bake each sheet, one at a time, for about 25 minutes, until the cookie tops begin to crack. Remove the baking sheet to a wire rack to cool for 5 minutes. Transfer cookies to a wire rack to cool completely. Continue baking in batches.

LEFT: *This unusual house jar would look great on any kitchen counter.*

Lacy Oatmeal Wafers

Makes about 2 dozen cookies

1 ½ cups quick-cooking
  oats
1 cup packed light
  brown sugar
½ cup superfine sugar
2 tablespoons all-purpose
  flour

¼ teaspoon salt
⅔ cup plus
  2 tablespoons
  unsalted butter, melted
1 egg, lightly beaten
1 teaspoon vanilla
  extract
½ cup mini chocolate
  chips (optional)

1. Preheat the oven to 350°F. In a large bowl, stir together the oats, sugars, flour, and salt. Make a well in the center of the mixture and add the melted butter, egg, and vanilla extract. Stir until well blended and a soft, batterlike dough forms. Stir in the chocolate chips, if using.

2. Drop teaspoonfuls of the mixture 2½ inches apart onto ungreased baking sheets. Bake for 3–5 minutes, until the edges are lightly brown and the centers are bubbling; the cookies will spread to form large disks. Remove the baking sheets to wire racks to cool slightly.

3. When the edges of the cookies are firm enough to lift, use a thin-bladed metal spatula to move them to wire racks to cool. Store in airtight containers, with waxed paper between each layer of cookies.

Coconut Macaroons

These delicious little cookies are perfect for those who can't eat wheat, as they contain no flour. **Makes about 2 dozen cookies**

3 cups sweetened,
  shredded coconut
1 cup unsalted
  macadamia nuts,
  chopped
Vegetable oil spray
  or vegetable oil,
  for greasing
2/3 cup sweetened
  condensed milk

1 teaspoon vanilla
  extract
2 egg whites
Pinch of salt

1. Preheat the oven to 350°F. Place the shredded coconut onto a large baking sheet and the macadamia nuts onto another baking sheet. Toast for 7–10 minutes, until lightly golden, stirring and shaking each sheet frequently. Pour the coconut onto a plate and the nuts onto another plate to cool completely.

2. Line two large baking sheets with nonstick baking

parchment, and spray or very lightly grease with oil. In a large bowl, stir together the condensed milk, vanilla extract, shredded coconut, and macadamia nuts until well blended.

3. In a medium bowl, using an electric mixer on medium speed, beat the egg whites until foamy. Add the salt and increase the mixer speed to high. Continue beating until the whites are stiff but not dry. Fold the egg whites into the coconut mixture. Drop rounded tablespoonfuls of the mixture onto the baking sheets and shape each mound into a cone. Bake for 10–12 minutes, until golden around the edges. Remove the baking sheets to wire racks to cool completely, then gently peel off the paper.

Banana Chocolate Chunkies

For the best results, use very ripe bananas for these dense, cakelike cookies.

Makes about 3 dozen cookies

1 1/2 cups all-purpose
  flour
1/2 cup whole-wheat
  flour
1/4 cup unsweetened
  cocoa powder
2 teaspoons baking
  powder
1/4 teaspoon baking soda
1/4 teaspoon ground
  cinnamon

1/2 teaspoon salt
6 oz. semisweet
  chocolate, chopped
3/4 cup (1 1/2 sticks)
  unsalted butter,
  softened
1/2 cup sugar
1/2 cup packed light
  brown sugar
1 cup mashed bananas
  (2 large, ripe bananas)

1 teaspoon vanilla
  extract
2 eggs, lightly beaten
1 cup semisweet
  chocolate chips
6 oz. good-quality
  white chocolate,
  chopped
1 cup coarsely chopped
  walnuts
1 cup golden raisins

 *Drop Cookies*

1. Line four large baking sheets with foil, shiny side up. In a large bowl, sift together the flours, cocoa powder, baking powder, baking soda, ground cinnamon, and salt. In a heatproof bowl placed over a saucepan of just simmering water, melt the semisweet chocolate until smooth, stirring frequently. Remove from the heat and allow the chocolate to cool slightly.

2. In a large bowl, using an electric mixer, beat the butter for about 1 minute, until creamy. Gradually add the sugars, mashed bananas, and vanilla extract, and beat until well blended. Gradually beat in the cooled melted chocolate and continue beating for 1–2 minutes, until the mixture lightens in color. Beat in the eggs until just blended.

3. Gently stir in the flour mixture, chocolate chips, chopped white chocolate, chopped walnuts, and golden raisins until well mixed. Using an ice cream scoop or ¼-cup measure, scoop up the cookie dough and use the side of the bowl to flatten the bottom of scoop or top of the measure. Drop, 3 inches apart, onto the foil-lined sheets. Moisten the bottom of a drinking glass and use to flatten each mound slightly. You will only get five or six cookies on a sheet. Refrigerate for 20 minutes.

4. Preheat the oven to 375°F. Bake the cookies, two sheets at a time, for 15–20 minutes, rotating baking sheets from the top and bottom shelves and front to back halfway through the cooking time; do not overbake.

The cookies are done when the top feels slightly firm to the touch. Remove the baking sheets to wire racks to cool for 2 minutes. Move each cookie to wire racks to cool completely. Repeat with the remaining prepared sheets; remove the remaining sheets of prepared cookies from the refrigerator 10 minutes before baking or the dough will be too cold. Store the cookies in large, airtight containers with waxed paper between the layers.

Walnut and Raisin Cookies

This old-fashioned recipe is based on Amish-style cookies, which are simple to bake and full of flavor. **Makes about 3 dozen cookies**

Vegetable oil spray
  or vegetable oil,
  for greasing
1 cup (2 sticks) butter
1 1/2 cups light brown
  sugar
3 eggs
1 teaspoon baking soda
  dissolved in 1 1/2
  tablespoons hot water

3 1/4 cups all-purpose
  flour
1/2 teaspoon salt
1 teaspoon ground
  cinnamon
1 cup chopped walnuts
1 cup golden raisins

 *Drop Cookies*

1. Preheat the oven to 350°F. Lightly spray or grease two large baking sheets. In a large bowl, using an electric mixer, beat the butter and sugar until light and fluffy. Beat in the eggs, one at a time.

2. Add the dissolved baking soda to the butter mixture, then stir in half the flour, the salt, and cinnamon. Stir in the walnuts, raisins, and the remaining flour until well blended.

3. Drop tablespoonfuls of the mixture at least 2 inches apart onto the baking sheets. Bake for 8–10 minutes, until golden. Remove the baking sheets to wire racks to cool slightly, then transfer the cookies to wire racks to cool completely. Repeat with remaining dough. Store in airtight containers.

RIGHT: *The Black Engine and Caboose cookie jar.*

Fruit 'n' Nut Oatmeal Cookies

Be sure to use old-fashioned rolled oats for a good texture in these chewy cookies. **Makes about 3 dozen cookies**

3 cups raisins

1 cup dried cranberries
or cherries

1 cup boiling water

Vegetable oil spray or
oil, for greasing

3/4 cup (1 1/2 sticks)
unsalted butter,
softened

1 1/2 cups packed light
brown sugar

2 eggs, lightly beaten

1 1/2 teaspoons vanilla
extract

2 1/2 cups all-purpose
flour

1/2 teaspoon baking
powder

1 1/2 teaspoons baking
soda

2 teaspoons ground
cinnamon

1 teaspoon ground ginger

1/2 teaspoon allspice

1/2 teaspoon salt

2 cups old-fashioned
rolled oats

2 cups chopped walnuts,
lightly toasted

1 1/2 cups pitted
prunes, chopped

1 cup pitted
dates, chopped

1. In a small bowl, combine the dried fruit. Pour in the boiling water and allow to stand, covered, for 15 minutes, stirring occasionally. Drain, reserving ⅓ cup of the soaking liquid, and set aside.

2. Preheat the oven to 400°F. Lightly spray or grease two large baking sheets. In a large bowl, using an electric mixer, beat the butter until creamy. Add the sugar and continue beating for about 2 minutes, until light and fluffy. Slowly beat in the eggs and vanilla extract.

3. Sift the flour, baking powder, baking soda, cinnamon, ginger, allspice, and salt into a large bowl. Stir in the butter mixture alternately with the reserved soaking liquid, until blended. Stir in the oats, walnuts, prunes, dates, and soaked raisins and cranberries.

4. Drop heaping tablespoonfuls onto the baking sheets, at least 3 inches apart. Flatten slightly with the back of a moistened spoon. Bake for 6–8 minutes, until golden and set. Remove the baking sheets to wire racks to cool slightly. Transfer the cookies to wire racks to cool. Repeat with the remaining dough. Store in an airtight container.

RIGHT: *Practical and cute, the Polka Dot Witch cookie jar is a modern classic.*

Hermits

If you wish, replace the allspice and raisins in this recipe with cinnamon and chopped nuts for another tasty version. **Makes about 50 cookies**

Vegetable oil spray
 or vegetable oil,
 for greasing
1/2 cup (1 stick) butter
1 cup sugar
1/2 cup milk
2 cups all-purpose
 flour
1 teaspoon allspice
1/2 teaspoon
 baking soda

1/2 teaspoon cream
 of tartar
2/3 cup raisins, chopped

1. Preheat the oven to 375°F. Lightly spray or grease two large baking sheets. In a large bowl, using an electric mixer, beat the butter and sugar together until light and fluffy. Gradually beat in the milk.

2. Sift the flour, allspice, baking soda, and cream of tartar into a bowl. Gradually add to the butter mixture, beating well after each addition, until smooth and well blended. Stir in the chopped raisins until well blended.

3. Drop teaspoonfuls of the mixture at least 2½ inches apart onto the baking sheets. Bake for 12–15 minutes, until golden brown. Remove the baking sheets to wire racks to cool slightly. Using a thin-bladed spatula, transfer to wire racks to cool completely. Repeat with the remaining mixture. Store in airtight containers.

LEFT: *The overalls-clad Smiley Pig was one of the most popular cookie jars produced by Shawnee.*

RIGHT: *New Wave Peanut Butter Cookies and Cream Cheese Macadamia Drops*

New Wave Peanut Butter Cookies

Peanut butter cookies have been traditional for decades, but these have extra peanuts and white chocolate. **Makes 18 cookies**

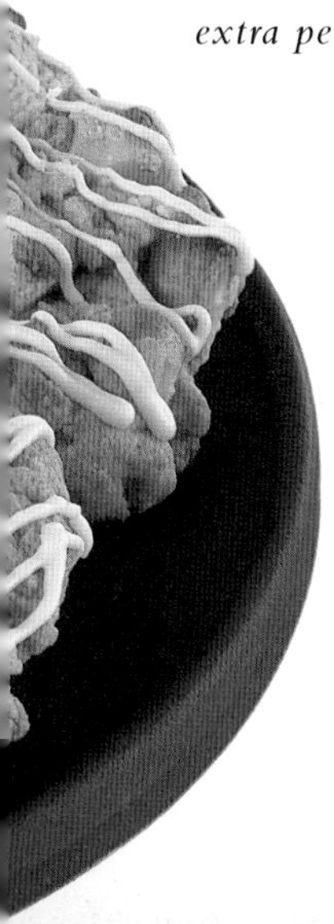

1 cup freshly shelled
  peanuts
Vegetable oil spray
  or vegetable oil,
  for greasing
1 cup all-purpose flour
1/2 teaspoon baking
  soda
1/4 teaspoon salt
1/2 cup chunky peanut
  butter

1/2 cup (1 stick) unsalted
  butter, softened
1/2 cup packed light
  brown sugar
2 tablespoons sugar
1 egg, lightly beaten
1 teaspoon vanilla
  extract
6 oz. white chocolate
  chips or white
  chocolate, chopped

1. Put the peanuts in a medium skillet or frying pan and toast over medium-low heat for about 5 minutes, until golden and fragrant, stirring frequently. Pour the nuts onto a plate and leave to cool.

2. Preheat the oven to 375°F. Lightly spray or grease two large baking sheets. Sift the flour, baking soda, and salt into a medium bowl. In a large bowl, using an electric mixer, beat the peanut butter, butter, and sugars together for 2–3 minutes, until light and fluffy. Gradually add the egg and continue beating for 2 minutes. Beat in the vanilla extract. Stir in the flour mixture until well blended, then stir in the chocolate and peanuts.

3. Drop heaping tablespoonfuls of the mixture at least 2 inches apart onto the baking sheets. Flatten slightly with the back of a moistened spoon. Bake for about 10 minutes, until golden brown. Do not overbake.

4. Remove the baking sheets to wire racks to cool for 5 minutes. Transfer the cookies to wire racks to cool completely. Store in an airtight container.

RIGHT: *Choose your favorite cookie tune from this wacky jukebox cookie jar made by Vandor.*

Cream Cheese Macadamia Drops

The macadamia nut is rich and creamy, and goes perfectly with the cream cheese base and white chocolate chunks in this recipe. **Makes about 20 cookies**

½ cup (1 stick) unsalted butter, softened

8 oz. cream cheese, softened

¾ cup packed light brown sugar

Grated zest of 1 lemon

1½ teaspoons vanilla extract

1½ cups all-purpose flour

2 teaspoons baking powder

1 cup coarsely chopped unsalted macadamia nuts

4 oz. white chocolate, coarsely chopped

Vegetable oil spray or vegetable oil, for greasing

6 oz. white chocolate, melted (optional)

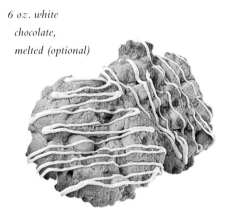

1. In a large bowl, using an electric mixer, beat the butter and cream cheese for 1–2 minutes, until creamy. Add the sugar and continue beating for 1–2 minutes, until light and fluffy. Beat in the lemon zest and vanilla extract.

2. Sift the flour and baking powder into a bowl, and stir into the cream cheese mixture.

RIGHT: *The Chef jar, typical of many made by the Regal China Company, has a subtle, homey appeal.*

Stir in the chopped nuts and chocolate. Chill the dough for about 30 minutes, until firm. **3.** Preheat the oven to 400°F. Lightly spray or grease two large baking sheets. Drop heaping teaspoonfuls of the mixture 2 inches apart onto the baking sheets and flatten slightly. Bake for 8–10 minutes, until puffed and golden. Remove the baking sheets to wire racks to cool for 5 minutes, then transfer the cookies to wire racks to cool completely. Repeat with the remaining mixture.

4. If you like, make a cone for piping the chocolate. Fold a square of waxed paper in half to form a triangle. With the triangle point facing you, fold the left corner down to the center. Fold the right corner down and wrap around the folded left corner. Fill the cone with the chocolate, then fold the top edges over to enclose it. Snip off the tip to make a hole $1/8$ inch in diameter. Pipe over the cookies in a zigzag pattern and allow to set.

New England–Style Jumbles

This chunky, old-fashioned American cookie was so called because of the nuts "jumbled" into the dough. The addition of dried cranberries and blueberries gives the cookies a real New England flavor. **Makes about 3 dozen cookies**

1 1/4 cups all-purpose
  flour
3/4 teaspoon baking soda
1/2 teaspoon ground
  cinnamon
1/8 teaspoon salt
1 cup semisweet
  chocolate chips
3/4 cup walnuts, coarsely
  chopped

3/4 cup hazelnuts,
  chopped
3/4 cup unblanched whole
  almonds, chopped
1 cup dried cranberries
1/4 cup dried sour cherries
1/2 cup dried blueberries
1/2 cup (1 stick) unsalted
  butter, softened
3/4 cup sugar

1/4 cup packed light
  brown sugar
1 egg
1 teaspoon vanilla
  extract

1. Preheat the oven to 375°F. In a medium bowl, sift together the flour, baking soda, cinnamon, and salt. In a large bowl, stir the chocolate chips, walnuts, hazelnuts, almonds, dried cranberries, cherries, and blueberries. **2.** In a large bowl, using an electric mixer, beat the butter for about 1 minute, until

LEFT: *The Metlox Cat is a "head" jar—a popular form of cookie jar inspired by everything from animal heads to those of cartoon characters.*

creamy. Add the sugars and beat for 1–2 minutes, until light and fluffy. Beat in the egg and vanilla extract. On low speed, beat in the flour mixture until blended, then stir in the nuts and dried fruits until combined.

3. Drop by rounded tablespoonfuls, 2 inches apart on two large, ungreased baking sheets. Bake for 12–15 minutes, until golden, rotating baking sheets between the top and bottom shelves, and from front to back, halfway through cooking time. Remove the baking sheets to wire racks to cool slightly. Move the cookies to wire racks to cool completely. Repeat with the remaining dough. Store in airtight containers.

TIP

○ **If the dough seems soft, refrigerate it for 15 minutes before dropping onto the baking sheets. This keeps the batter from spreading too much.**

Sesame Thins

These are sweet, crisp wafers, rich with the flavor of sesame. They make an unusual accompaniment to sorbets and ice cream desserts. **Makes about 3 dozen cookies**

½ cup sesame seeds
1 tablespoon butter
1 cup packed light
brown sugar

3 tablespoons flour
Pinch of salt
1 egg, lightly beaten
1 teaspoon vanilla
extract

1. Preheat the oven to 350°F. Generously grease two large baking sheets. In a medium pan over medium heat, toast the sesame seeds, stirring and shaking the pan until they are golden and fragrant. Remove the pan from the heat, cool slightly, then stir in the remaining ingredients until well blended.

2. Drop teaspoonfuls of the mixture 2½ inches apart onto the baking sheets. Bake 3–5 minutes, until just golden. Remove the baking sheets to wire racks to cool slightly.

3. When an edge is firm enough to lift, use a thin palette knife to move the cookies to wire racks to cool completely. Repeat with the remaining mixture, cooling and regreasing the baking sheets between each batch. Store these fragile cookies in an airtight container with waxed paper between each layer.

RIGHT: *The wonderful expression on the face of this calf is typical of the appeal of many cookie jars.*

Triple Chocolate Chip Cookies

This is a slightly updated version of the classic chocolate chip cookie—more chocolatey and chunky than ever. **Makes about 4 dozen cookies**

2 ¼ cups all-purpose
   flour
1 teaspoon baking soda
¾ teaspoon salt
1 cup (2 sticks) unsalted
   butter or margarine,
   softened
1 cup packed light brown
   sugar
½ cup sugar
2 eggs

1 teaspoon vanilla
   extract
12 oz. semisweet
   chocolate chips or
   semisweet chocolate,
   finely chopped
6 oz. good-quality
   milk chocolate, chopped
6 oz. good-quality
   white chocolate,
   chopped

1 cup chopped pecans
   or walnuts

 *Drop Cookies*

1. Preheat the oven to 375°F. In a large bowl, stir together the flour, baking soda, and salt. In another large bowl, with an electric mixer, beat the butter and sugars for about 2 minutes, until light and fluffy. With the mixer on low speed, beat in the eggs and vanilla, beating well after each addition and scraping down the sides of the bowl occasionally. Stir in the flour mixture, chocolate chips, chopped chocolate, and nuts until a well-blended dough forms.

2. Drop rounded tablespoonfuls of the mixture onto two large, ungreased baking sheets, at least 2 inches apart. Bake for 10–12 minutes, until set and golden brown, rotating baking sheets between the top and bottom shelves, and from front to back, halfway through cooking time. Remove baking sheets to wire racks to cool slightly. Using a palette knife, move the cookies to wire racks to cool completely. Repeat with remaining dough. Store in an airtight container.

Refrigerator & Rolled *cookies*

Coconut Lime Squares

These cookies have a distinctly coconut flavor. If you like, add a few drops of rum extract instead of almond for a more Caribbean flavor. **Makes about 3 dozen**

2 cups plus
2 tablespoons
 all-purpose flour
1/2 teaspoon salt
1 cup (2 sticks) unsalted
 butter, softened
1 cup sugar
2 eggs, lightly beaten
Grated zest of 1 lime
1/2 teaspoon vanilla
 extract

1/2 teaspoon almond
 extract
1 tablespoon lime juice
3/4 cup sweetened,
 shredded coconut,
 plus extra for
 decorating
Vegetable oil spray
 or vegetable oil,
 for greasing

1. Sift the flour and salt into a medium bowl. In a large bowl, beat the butter for 30 seconds, until creamy. Add the sugar and continue beating for 1–2 minutes, until light and fluffy. Beat in the eggs, lime zest, vanilla and almond extracts, and lime juice until well blended. Stir in the flour and shredded coconut.

2. Divide the dough in half and scrape onto two pieces of plastic wrap or waxed paper. Using the wrap or paper as a guide, form each dough half into a log about 2 inches in diameter. Flatten slightly on all sides to make a "square" log shape. Wrap tightly and refrigerate for several hours or overnight, until firm. The cookie dough can be made up to five days ahead, or frozen.

3. Preheat the oven to 375°F. Lightly spray or grease two large baking sheets. Unwrap and, with a sharp knife, cut the dough log into ¼-inch slices. Place the slices 1 inch apart on the baking sheets. Sprinkle each cookie

with a little shredded coconut. Bake for about 10 minutes, until just golden. Remove the baking sheets to wire racks to cool slightly, then transfer the cookies onto wire racks to cool completely. Repeat with the remaining dough slices. Store in airtight containers.

RIGHT: *This endearing and very collectable dalmatian jar was made by McCoy, one of the most prolific cookie jar manufacturers.*

97

Raspberry Jam Sandwiches

Ground almonds make an especially fine-textured cookie dough.
These tender cookie squares can be filled with any flavor jam.

Makes about 18 cookies

1 1/4 cups blanched
  almonds
1 1/2 cups all-purpose
  flour
3/4 cup (1 1/2 sticks)
  salted butter, softened
1/2 cup superfine sugar
1 egg, separated
Grated zest of 1 lemon

1 teaspoon vanilla
  extract
1/2 teaspoon salt
1/2 cup slivered almonds
1 cup raspberry jam
1 tablespoon lemon
  juice
Confectioners' sugar, to
  dust (optional)

1. Put the blanched almonds and ¼ cup of the flour in the bowl of a food processor and process until very finely ground.

2. In a large bowl, using an electric mixer, beat the butter for about 30 seconds, until creamy. Add the sugar and continue beating for 1–2 minutes, until light and fluffy. Beat in the egg yolk, lemon zest, and vanilla extract until well blended. On low speed, beat in the almond mixture, the remaining flour, and salt until well blended.

3. Scrape the dough onto a sheet of waxed paper or plastic wrap and, using the paper or wrap as a guide, form into a flat disk. Refrigerate for 2 hours or overnight, until firm enough to handle. The dough can be made up to two days ahead.

4. Preheat the oven to 350°F. Line two baking sheets with nonstick baking parchment. On a lightly floured surface, using a floured rolling pin, roll half the dough into a 12-inch square. Keep the remaining dough refrigerated. Cut the square crosswise into six strips, then lengthwise into six strips to make thirty-six 2-inch squares. Using a floured ¾-inch round cookie cutter, cut out the centers from half the squares.

5. Transfer the squares to the baking sheets ½ inch apart. In a small bowl, whisk the egg white until frothy. Brush the top of the cookie rings only, then sprinkle each ring with a few slivered almonds. Bake for 8–10 minutes, until just golden. Remove the baking sheets to a wire rack to cool slightly, then transfer the cookies to wire racks to cool completely. (If you like, dust the rings with confectioners' sugar.) Repeat with the remaining dough and trimmings.

6. In a small saucepan over low heat, heat the jam and lemon juice until melted. Spoon over the squares, then top with a cookie ring, pressing gently. Allow to set, then store in airtight containers with waxed paper between the layers.

Christmas Cutout Cookies

Use this lemony sugar cookie as a base to form lots of Christmas shapes. Look for interesting cookie cutters, from angels to reindeers. **Makes about 6 dozen cookies**

2 cups all-purpose flour

2 teaspoons baking powder

1/2 teaspoon salt

1/2 cup (1 stick) unsalted butter, softened

1 cup superfine sugar

1 egg, lightly beaten

Grated zest of 1 lemon

1 tablespoon lemon juice

1 tablespoon vanilla extract

1/2 teaspoon lemon extract

3 cups confectioners' sugar

2–3 tablespoons milk

1 tablespoon lemon juice

Red and green food coloring (optional)

1. Sift the flour, baking powder, and salt into a medium bowl. In a large bowl, using an electric mixer, beat the butter for about 30 seconds, until creamy. Add the sugar and

continue beating for 1–2 minutes, until light and fluffy. Beat in the egg, lemon zest and juice, and vanilla and lemon extracts, then stir in the flour mixture until well blended and a soft dough forms.

2. Form the dough into a ball and flatten to a disk shape. Wrap tightly and refrigerate for several hours or overnight, until the dough is firm enough to handle.

3. Preheat the oven to 350°F. On a lightly floured surface, using a floured rolling pin, roll out one third of the dough ⅛ inch thick. Keep the remaining dough refrigerated. Using floured cookie cutters, cut out as many shapes as possible and place them 1 inch apart on two large, ungreased baking sheets.

4. Bake for about 8 minutes, until the cookies are just colored around the edges. Use a spatula to transfer the cookies to wire racks to cool completely. Repeat with the remaining dough.

5. Sift the confectioners' sugar into a bowl and stir in 2 tablespoons of milk and lemon juice, adding a little more milk if the icing is too thick. Spoon about one third of the icing into a bowl and another third into another bowl. Mix a few drops of red coloring into one bowl and green into the other.

6. Spoon each color into a paper cone (see page 81). Pipe designs onto each shape. Allow to set for 2 hours. Store in airtight containers, with waxed paper between the layers.

Poppy Seed Spirals

Poppy seed paste is a popular filling in many German and Austrian coffee cakes. Here it is used in these deliciously crisp cookie spirals. **Makes about 4 dozen cookies**

1/2 cup walnut pieces,
  finely ground
1/2 cup poppy seeds
1/3 cup honey
1/2 teaspoon ground
  cinnamon

LEFT: *This quirky character is Pierre, one of many chef cookie jars.*

Grated zest of 1 orange
6 tablespoons unsalted
  butter, softened
1/2 cup superfine sugar
1 egg, lightly beaten
1 teaspoon rum extract
1 1/2 cups all-purpose
  flour
Vegetable oil spray or
  oil, for greasing

1. In a small bowl, combine the ground walnuts, poppy seeds, honey, cinnamon, orange zest, and 2 tablespoons of softened butter to form a paste. Set aside.

2. In a large bowl, using an electric mixer, beat the remaining butter and sugar for 1–2 minutes, until light and fluffy. Beat in the egg and rum extract until well blended, then slowly stir in the flour until a soft dough forms. Refrigerate the dough for 15–20 minutes, until firm enough to handle.

3. On a lightly floured sheet of waxed paper or nonstick baking parchment, roll out the dough to a rectangle about ¼ inch thick and spread with the poppy seed paste. Starting at one short side, roll up the dough, jelly-roll fashion, and wrap tightly in plastic wrap or foil. Refrigerate for several hours or overnight, until firm. The dough can be refrigerated for up to five days or frozen.

4. Preheat the oven to 375°F. Lightly spray or grease two large, nonstick baking sheets.

Unwrap and slice the dough roll crosswise into ¼-inch slices and place ½ inch apart on the baking sheets. Bake for about 10 minutes, until golden; do not overbake. Remove the baking sheets to wire racks. Using a spatula, transfer the cookies to wire racks to cool. Repeat with the remaining slices. Store in airtight containers.

RIGHT: *With cookie in hand, this pink hippo jar from Fitz and Floyd tempts the sweet-toothed.*

Chocolate-Drizzled Almond Cookies

This is a traditional cookie found in Belgium. Rolling the dough log in chopped almonds and drizzling the baked cookies with dark chocolate adds a new dimension.

Makes about 3 dozen cookies

3 tablespoons unsalted
  butter
1/4 cup milk
2 tablespoons brandy
2 cups all-purpose flour
1/2 teaspoon baking
  powder
3/4 teaspoon ground
  cinnamon
1/4 teaspoon salt

1 cup blanched almonds,
  grated or very finely
  chopped
1/2 cup packed light
  brown sugar
1 cup blanched almonds,
  finely chopped
6 oz. semisweet
  chocolate, melted

1. In a small saucepan over low heat, melt the butter. Remove from heat, cool slightly, and stir in the milk and brandy. Set aside.

2. In a large bowl, sift together the flour, baking powder, cinnamon, and salt. Stir in the grated or finely chopped almonds and sugar, then stir into the butter mixture to form a soft dough.

3. Scrape the dough onto a piece of plastic wrap or waxed paper and, using the wrap or paper as a guide, form the dough into a log 2 inches thick. Chill the log for 5–10 minutes. Sprinkle the chopped almonds on a work surface and roll the dough log in them, pressing the almonds into the surface of the dough. Rewrap the log and refrigerate for several hours or overnight, until firm.

4. Preheat the oven to 375°F. Lightly grease two large baking sheets. Cut the log crosswise into ½-inch slices and place 1 inch apart on the baking sheets. Bake for about 10 minutes, until golden. Remove the cookies to wire racks to cool.

5. Arrange the cookies close together. Spoon the melted chocolate into a paper cone (see page 81) and drizzle the chocolate over the cookies. Alternatively, use a teaspoon to drizzle the chocolate. Allow to set, then store in an airtight container, with waxed paper between the layers.

Cashew Butter Cookies

Cashew butter is available at some health food stores, but it's easy to make your own with a food processor. It's worth it—these cookies have a rich texture and intense flavor.

Makes about 4 dozen cookies

1 cup unsalted, roasted
  cashews
2 tablespoons
  vegetable oil
1²/₃ cups all-purpose
  flour
1 teaspoon baking soda
¹/₂ teaspoon salt
¹/₂ cup (1 stick) unsalted
  butter, softened

¹/₂ cup sugar
¹/₂ cup packed light
  brown sugar
1 egg, lightly beaten
1 teaspoon vanilla
  extract
¹/₂ teaspoon rum extract
1 cup chopped, roasted
  cashews
¹/₂ cup old-fashioned oats

1. In a food processor fitted with a metal blade, process the cashews and vegetable oil until a thick paste forms, similar to peanut butter. In a medium bowl, sift together the flour, baking soda, and salt.

2. In a large bowl, using an electric mixer, beat the butter and sugars for 1–2 minutes, until light and fluffy. Gradually beat in the egg, cashew butter, and vanilla and rum extracts until well blended.

3. On low speed, beat the flour into the cashew butter mixture until a soft dough forms. Stir in the chopped cashew nuts and oats until thoroughly mixed. On a lightly floured surface, form the dough into two 2-inch logs. Wrap each log tightly in plastic wrap or waxed paper and refrigerate for 4–6 hours or overnight, until firm.

4. Preheat the oven to 300°F. Lightly grease two large baking sheets. Cut the dough log crosswise into 1/2-inch slices and place 1 inch apart on baking sheets. Bake until golden, about 10 minutes. Remove baking sheets to wire racks to cool slightly. Using a metal spatula, remove the cookies to wire racks to cool completely. Repeat with remaining dough or freeze for future use. Store in airtight containers.

RIGHT: *"Happy" and "Cookie" were manufactured by Shawnee in the 1930s and 1940s. One of the most popular cookie jar manufacturers, Shawnee jars are highly collectible.*

115

Chocolate-Orange Stars

To make these pretty cookies, you need three cutters of the same shape, about 3¼, 2⅛ and 1 inch in diameter. They are surprisingly simple to make once you get going. **Makes about 30 cookies**

2 oz. semisweet
   chocolate, chopped
2 ¼ cups all-purpose
   flour
1 ½ teaspoons
   baking powder
¼ teaspoon salt
¾ cup (1 ½ sticks)
   unsalted butter,
   softened

¾ cup sugar
1 egg
1 teaspoon vanilla
   extract
Grated zest of
   1 orange
1 tablespoon orange
   juice
Superfine sugar, for
   sprinkling

1. Place the chocolate in a small bowl and set over a small saucepan of hot water. Melt over low heat until smooth, stirring frequently.

2. In a medium bowl, sift together the flour, baking powder, and salt. In a large bowl, using an electric mixer, beat the butter and sugar until light and creamy. Beat in the egg, vanilla extract, orange zest, and juice. On low speed, beat in the flour until a soft dough forms. Remove half the dough, wrap tightly, and refrigerate until firm, about 2 hours.

3. With the mixer on low speed, beat the melted, cooled chocolate into the remaining dough until no streaks of chocolate remain. Wrap the dough and refrigerate until firm, about 2 hours.

4. Grease and flour two or more large baking sheets. On a lightly floured surface, using a floured rolling pin, roll out half the orange-flavored dough ⅛ inch thick (keep remaining dough refrigerated). With a floured 3¼-inch star-shaped cutter, cut out as many stars as possible. Place ½ inch apart on a baking sheet. Repeat with the remaining dough and refrigerate. Repeat with the chocolate dough, cutting an equal amount of chocolate stars and place on another baking sheet. Refrigerate about 20 minutes, until firm.

5. Preheat the oven to 350°F. With a floured 2⅛-inch star-shaped cutter, cut another star from the center of each 3¼-inch star. Place smaller orange stars in larger chocolate stars and smaller chocolate stars in larger orange stars. With a 1-inch star cutter, cut small stars from the center of each cookie and put small orange stars into medium chocolate stars and small chocolate stars into medium orange stars to create alternating colors.

6. Sprinkle the cookies with a little superfine sugar and bake for about 10 minutes, until golden. Remove the baking sheets to wire racks and move the cookies to wire racks to cool completely. Store the cookies in airtight containers.

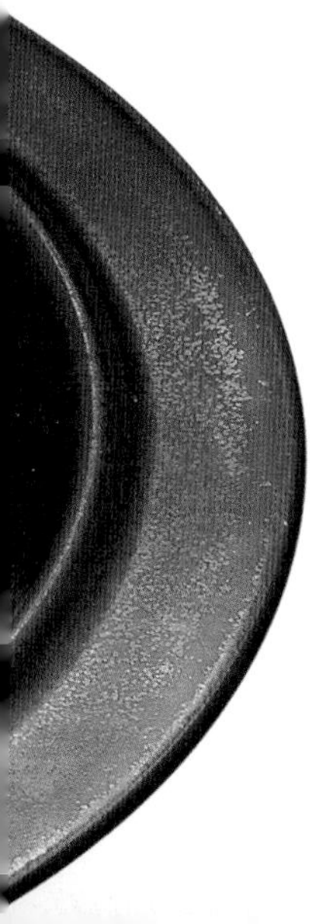

Sand Tarts

*The name of these sugar-rich cookies comes from their
grainy or sandy texture.* **Makes about 3 dozen cookies**

Butter or vegetable oil,
  for greasing
1 ¼ cups sugar
1 cup (2 sticks) butter
1 egg, beaten
2 cups all-purpose
  flour

1 egg white,
  lightly beaten
Sugar
Finely chopped
  pecans or
  walnuts

1. In a large bowl, using an electric mixer, beat the sugar and butter until light and fluffy. Beat in the egg. On low speed, gradually beat in the flour until a stiff dough forms. Shape into a ball and flatten to a disk shape. Wrap the dough in plastic wrap and refrigerate overnight or until firm.

2. Preheat the oven to 350°F. Butter or oil two large baking sheets. Cut the dough into four pieces and refrigerate all but one piece of the dough. On a lightly floured surface, using a lightly floured rolling pin, roll out the unrefrigerated dough about ¼ inch thick. Using a 2- or 3-inch cutter, cut out as many rounds as possible.

3. Place the rounds on the baking sheets, brush the tops with the beaten egg white, and sprinkle with a mixture of sugar and nuts. Bake for about 10 minutes, until set and pale golden. Remove the baking sheets to wire racks to cool for 2 minutes. Using a metal spatula, transfer the cookies to wire racks to cool completely. Repeat with the remaining pieces of dough. Store in airtight containers.

RIGHT: *This jolly-looking cookie jar is the Tuggle Tuggle Tugboat, made by Sierra Vista.*

CLOCKWISE FROM
RIGHT: *Moravian
Spice Squares,
Chocolate Pistachio
Pinwheels, and
Shrewsbury
Biscuits*

Moravian Spice Squares

Makes about 30 cookies

¼ cup (½ stick)
  unsalted butter
¼ cup packed dark
  brown sugar
2 tablespoons molasses
1 ¼ cups all-purpose
  flour
Grated zest of 1 lemon
1 teaspoon ground ginger
1 teaspoon ground
  cinnamon

¼ teaspoon ground
  cloves
½ teaspoon baking
  soda
Vegetable oil spray
  or vegetable oil,
  for greasing
Sugar, for
  sprinkling

1. In a medium saucepan, gently heat the butter, brown sugar, and molasses until melted and smooth, stirring often. Remove from the heat and blend in the flour, lemon zest, ginger, cinnamon, cloves, and baking soda.

2. Scrape the dough onto a piece of waxed paper or plastic wrap and shape into a flat disk. Wrap tightly and refrigerate for several hours or overnight.

3. Preheat the oven to 350°F. Lightly spray or grease two large baking sheets. On a lightly floured surface, using a floured rolling pin, roll half of the dough into a 10-inch square. Using a sharp knife or pastry cutter, cut the dough into 1¼-inch squares and place 1 inch apart on the baking sheet.

4. With a fork, gently prick the cookies to keep them from puffing up, and sprinkle with sugar. Bake for 7 minutes, until just set. Using a spatula, transfer to wire racks to cool completely. Repeat with the remaining dough. Store in airtight containers.

LEFT: *The Old Lady in the Shoe is just one of many jars featuring nursery rhyme characters.*

Chocolate Pistachio Pinwheels

Makes about 3 dozen cookies

2½ cups all-purpose
   flour
2 tablespoons
   unsweetened cocoa
   powder
2½ teaspoons baking
   powder
½ teaspoon salt
½ cup (1 stick) unsalted
   butter, softened
½ cup superfine sugar

1 egg, lightly beaten
2 tablespoons light corn
   syrup
Vegetable oil spray
   or vegetable oil,
   for greasing
1½ cups finely
   chopped pistachio or
   macadamia nuts

1. Sift the flour, cocoa powder, baking powder, and salt into a medium bowl.

2. In a large bowl, using an electric mixer, beat the butter and sugar for 1–2 minutes, until light and creamy. Beat in the egg and corn syrup until blended, then stir in the flour mixture. Turn the dough onto a lightly floured surface and knead lightly until smooth. Wrap tightly in plastic wrap or waxed paper and refrigerate for about 30 minutes, until firm enough to roll.

3. Preheat the oven to 350°F. Lightly spray or grease two large baking sheets. On a lightly floured surface, using a floured rolling pin, roll out half the dough ⅛ inch thick. Keep the remaining dough refrigerated. Using a floured 3½-inch round or square cutter, cut out rounds or squares.

4. Place the cutouts on the baking sheets. With a knife, and beginning at the outside edge, make four cuts almost to the center to form quarters (if a square cutter has been used, make a diagonal cut from each corner). Fold the right corner of each quarter to the center and press to seal, forming a pinwheel shape. Sprinkle the center with the nuts.

5. Bake for about 10 minutes, until firm. Remove the sheets to wire racks to cool slightly. Transfer the cookies to wire racks to cool completely.

Shrewsbury Biscuits

These traditional English cookies have a rich, buttery texture.

Makes about 3 dozen cookies

1 cup (2 sticks) unsalted
  butter
1 cup superfine sugar
1 egg, beaten
¼ cup heavy cream
1 tablespoon dry
  sherry
½ cup currants
1–1¼ cups all-
  purpose flour,
  sifted

Superfine sugar,
  for sprinkling

1. In a large bowl, using an electric mixer, beat the butter and sugar for 1–2 minutes, until light and creamy. Beat in the egg, cream, sherry, and currants. Stir in the flour until a soft dough forms.

2. Scrape out onto plastic wrap and, using the wrap as a guide, shape into a flat disk. Refrigerate for 1 hour, until firm.

3. Preheat the oven to 350°F. Grease two large baking sheets.

On a lightly floured surface, roll out the dough ¼ inch thick. With a 2½-inch cutter, cut out rounds. Place 1 inch apart on baking sheets.

4. Brush with water and sprinkle with a little superfine sugar. Bake for about 15 minutes, until crisp and just beginning to brown. Remove the baking sheets to wire racks to cool slightly. Using a thin-bladed metal spatula, transfer the cookies to wire racks to cool completely. Store in airtight containers.

Hazelnut Marmalade Swirls

These two-tone refrigerator cookies combine an orange-scented dough with a delicious marmalade-chocolate-hazelnut filling.

Makes about 4 dozen cookies

1 cup hazelnuts, toasted
   and finely ground
1/2 cup orange
   marmalade
2 oz. semisweet
   chocolate, grated
1/2 teaspoon ground
   cinnamon
1/4 teaspoon grated
   nutmeg

Grated zest of 1 orange
1 cup plus 3 tablespoons
   packed light brown
   sugar
1/4 cup (1/2 stick) butter
   or margarine
1/4 cup vegetable
   shortening
1 3/4 cups all-purpose
   flour

1 egg
Vegetable oil spray
   or vegetable oil,
   for greasing
4 oz. semisweet
   chocolate, melted

1. In a medium bowl, combine the ground hazelnuts, orange marmalade, grated chocolate, cinnamon, nutmeg, 1 tablespoon of the orange zest, and 3 tablespoons of the sugar, mixing thoroughly until a spreadable paste forms.

2. In a medium bowl, using an electric mixer, beat the butter or margarine, shortening, flour, egg, remaining sugar, and remaining orange zest until a stiff dough forms. Divide the dough in half.

3. On a piece of plastic wrap or waxed paper, roll out one piece of dough to a rectangle ¼ inch thick and spread with half the nut mixture. Starting at one short side, carefully roll up the dough, jelly-roll fashion, and wrap tightly. Repeat with the remaining dough and nut mixture. Refrigerate for several hours or overnight. The dough can be refrigerated for up to five days or frozen.

4. Preheat the oven to 350°F. Lightly spray or grease two large baking sheets. Unwrap one dough roll and cut crosswise into ¼-inch slices. Place the slices 1 inch apart on the baking sheets and bake for about 10 minutes, until golden. Remove the baking sheets to wire racks and, using a spatula, transfer the cookies to wire racks to cool. Repeat with the remaining dough roll. When the cookies are cool, drizzle each with a little melted chocolate and allow to set. Store in airtight containers.

Chocolate Mint Sandwiches

*This cookie is a luscious combination of mint-flavored white-chocolate filling sandwiched
between cocoa-cookie wafers, then glazed with chocolate.* **Makes about 2 dozen cookies**

1 cup all-purpose flour
*¼ cup unsweetened cocoa
   powder*
*½ cup (1 stick) unsalted
   butter, softened*
¼ cup sugar
1 egg, lightly beaten
1 teaspoon mint extract

CHOCOLATE FILLING
½ cup whipping cream
*7 oz. white
   chocolate, chopped*
1 teaspoon mint extract

GLAZE
*5 oz. bittersweet
   chocolate, chopped*
*3 oz. unsalted butter,
   cut into pieces*

1. In a medium bowl, sift together the flour
and cocoa powder. In a large bowl, using an
electric mixer, beat the butter and sugar for
1–2 minutes, until light and fluffy. Gradually
beat in the egg and mint extract until
blended. On low speed, beat in the flour
and cocoa mixture until a soft dough forms.
2. Scrape the dough onto a piece of plastic
wrap or waxed paper and, using the wrap or
paper as a guide, shape the dough into a flat
disk. Wrap tightly and refrigerate 1–2 hours

or overnight, until firm. The dough can be made up to two days ahead.

3. Preheat the oven to 350°F. Lightly grease two large baking sheets. On a lightly floured surface, using a floured rolling pin, roll out half the dough to ⅛ inch, or thinner if possible. With a 2½-inch floured cookie cutter, cut out as many cookies as possible. (Be sure to end up with an even number.)

4. Bake for 6–8 minutes, until edges are just set; do not overbake, as the cookies may dry

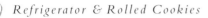

out or burn. Remove the baking sheets to wire racks to cool slightly. Using a metal spatula, move the cookies to wire racks to cool. Repeat with the remaining dough and trimmings.

5. In a medium saucepan over medium heat, bring the whipping cream to a boil. Remove from the heat and add the white chocolate all

LEFT: *The nostalgic look of this Cat on a Beehive cookie jar is a much-loved characteristic of many jars.*

at once, stirring constantly until melted and smooth. Stir in the mint extract and strain into a bowl. Cool until firm but not hard, about 1 hour, stirring occasionally to prevent a skin from forming.

6. Using a small palette knife, spread a little filling onto half of the cookies and immediately cover with another cookie, pressing together gently. Continue until all the cookies are sandwiched. Allow to set for 2 hours at room temperature.

7. In a small saucepan over low heat, melt the chocolate and butter, stirring until smooth. Remove the mixture from the heat and cool for 20–30 minutes, until thickened to spreading consistency. Using a small palette knife, carefully spread a small amount of the chocolate glaze on top of each sandwiched cookie, smoothing the tops. Refrigerate until set, 20–30 minutes. Store in airtight containers, refrigerated, with waxed paper between the layers.

Cheddar Pennies

Although not a sweet cookie, these spicy cheese rounds make an easy homemade snack. They are usually served with a drink and offer a nice change from peanuts and chips. **Makes about 4 dozen**

1/2 cup (1 stick) unsalted
  butter, softened
1 cup grated medium
  or sharp cheddar
  cheese
2/3 cup all-purpose
  flour
3 tablespoons fresh,
  chopped chives
1/8 teaspoon salt

1/4–1/2 teaspoon cayenne
  pepper or chili
  powder

1. In a large bowl, using an electric mixer, beat the butter for about 1 minute, until creamy. Stir in the grated cheese, flour, chives, salt, and cayenne pepper or chili powder to form a soft dough.

2. Scrape the dough onto a piece of plastic wrap or waxed paper and, using the wrap or paper as a guide, form into a long log about 1½ inches in diameter (if you prefer, make smaller pennies by forming the dough into a 1-inch log). Wrap tightly and refrigerate for several hours or overnight, until firm. The dough can be made up to five days ahead or frozen.

TIP
○ **This is a good way to use up small pieces of hard cheese, such as cheddar or Monterey Jack, but they should be well flavored and not bland to ensure a good flavor.**

3. Preheat the oven to 350°F. Lightly grease two large baking sheets. With a sharp knife, cut the dough log (or logs) into ¼-inch slices and place on prepared baking sheets. Bake for 10–12 minutes, until slightly puffed and golden. Using a metal spatula, move the cookies to a wire rack to cool. Store in an airtight container.

RIGHT: *This Howdy Doody cookie jar from Vandor is a "character jar" as well as a "head jar."*

Gingery Chocolate Cookies

Using fresh ginger gives these cookies a definite zing. The dough can be frozen for up to two months, then sliced and baked without defrosting. **Makes about 3 dozen cookies**

2–3-inch piece of fresh
  ginger, peeled
2 ½ cups all-purpose
  flour
2 tablespoons
  unsweetened cocoa
  powder (preferably
  Dutch-processed)
½ teaspoon ground
  ginger

½ teaspoon salt
¼ teaspoon finely
  ground black pepper
1 cup (2 sticks) unsalted
  butter, softened
1 cup packed dark
  brown sugar
2 egg yolks
2 teaspoons vanilla
  extract

12 oz. bittersweet
  or semisweet
  chocolate, chopped
Chopped candied
  ginger, to decorate

1. Grate the piece of ginger against the small, round holes of a cheese grater and set aside. Sift the flour, cocoa powder, ground ginger, salt, and pepper into a medium bowl.

2. In a large bowl, using an electric mixer, beat the butter for 30 seconds, until creamy. Add the brown sugar and continue beating for 1–2 minutes, until light and fluffy. Beat in the egg yolks and vanilla extract until the mixture is smooth. Stir in the flour mixture until blended.

3. Scrape the dough onto a piece of plastic wrap and, using the wrap as a guide, shape it into a 2½-inch log. Wrap tightly and refrigerate for 3–4 hours, or freeze until hard.

4. Preheat the oven to 350°F. Line two large baking sheets with nonstick baking parchment. Unwrap the dough and, using a sharp knife, cut the log into ¼-inch slices. Place 1 inch apart on the baking sheets.

5. Bake for about 12 minutes, until lightly browned, rotating the baking sheets between

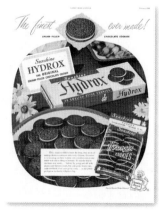

the top and bottom shelves, and from front to back, halfway through the cooking time. Remove the baking sheets to wire racks to cool for about 1 minute. Using a metal spatula, transfer the cookies to wire racks to cool completely.

6. Put the chocolate in a bowl and place over a pan of barely simmering water.

Stir until the chocolate melts. Set aside to cool, stirring occasionally. When the chocolate reaches a spreading consistency, use a small spoon to swirl a little on top of each cookie. Sprinkle with a little candied ginger and allow the cookies to set. Store in airtight containers, with waxed paper between the layers.

Coconut Crisps

These easy-to-make cookies have a subtle flavor, making them ideal to serve with chocolate desserts and fruit salads. **Makes about 5 dozen cookies**

2 cups plus
2 tablespoons
all-purpose flour
½ teaspoon salt
1 cup (2 sticks) unsalted
butter, softened
1 cup superfine sugar
2 eggs, lightly beaten
½ teaspoon
vanilla extract

½ teaspoon almond
extract
¾ cup sweetened
shredded coconut, plus
extra for garnish

1. In a medium bowl, sift the flour and salt. In a large bowl, using an electric mixer, beat the butter for about 1 minute, until creamy. Add the sugar and continue beating for 1–2 minutes, until light and fluffy. Slowly beat in the eggs and vanilla and almond extracts, then stir in the flour and shredded coconut until well blended.

2. Divide the dough in half and scrape onto two pieces of plastic wrap or waxed paper. Using the wrap or paper as a guide, form each dough half into a log about 2 inches in diameter. Wrap the dough logs tightly and refrigerate for several hours or overnight, until firm. The dough can be made up to five days ahead or frozen.

3. Preheat the oven to 375°F. Lightly grease two large baking sheets. Using a sharp knife, cut one dough log into ¼-inch slices. Place the slices about 1 inch apart on the prepared baking sheets and sprinkle each of the slices with a little shredded coconut.

4. Bake for 8–10 minutes, until just golden. Remove the baking sheets to wire racks to cool slightly. Using a metal spatula, move the cookies to wire racks to cool completely. Repeat with the remaining dough log or freeze for future use. Store in airtight containers.

Spicy Gingerbread Cactus

Gingerbread cookies probably originated in Germany or Austria, where elaborate gingerbread houses are used as festive decorations. **Makes about 2 dozen cookies**

3 1/2 cups all-purpose
  flour
1 teaspoon salt
1 teaspoon baking
  powder
1 1/2 teaspoons ground
  ginger
1 1/2 teaspoons ground
  cinnamon
1 1/2 teaspoons allspice
1 teaspoon ground cloves

1/2 teaspoon cayenne
  pepper, or to taste
1 cup (2 sticks) unsalted
  butter, softened
2/3 cup packed dark
  brown sugar
1/2 cup light molasses
1 egg, lightly beaten
Vegetable oil spray
  or vegetable oil,
  for greasing

ROYAL ICING
2 1/2 cups confectioners'
  sugar
1/4 teaspoon cream of
  tartar
2 egg whites
Food coloring (optional)
1 tablespoon lemon
  juice or rum

1. Sift the flour, salt, baking powder, ginger, cinnamon, allspice, cloves, and cayenne pepper into a medium bowl and set aside.

2. In another bowl, using an electric mixer, beat the butter and brown sugar for 1–2 minutes, until light and fluffy. Beat in the molasses and egg until blended. On low speed, beat in the flour mixture until a soft dough forms.

3. Scrape the dough onto a piece of plastic wrap or waxed paper and, using the wrap or paper, shape into a flat disk. Wrap tightly and refrigerate for several hours or overnight, until firm enough to roll. The dough can be made up to two days ahead.

4. Preheat the oven to 350°F. Lightly spray or grease two large baking sheets. On a lightly floured surface, using a floured rolling pin, roll half the dough ¼ inch thick. Keep the remaining dough refrigerated. Using a floured cutter, cut out as many cookies as possible. Arrange 1 inch apart on the baking sheets.

5. Bake for about 10 minutes, until the edges of the cookies are lightly browned. Remove the baking sheets to wire racks. Transfer the cookies to wire racks to cool completely. Repeat with the remaining cookie dough and dough trimmings.

6. Sift the confectioners' sugar and cream of tartar into a medium bowl. Using an electric

RIGHT: *Fred Flintstone is one of the many cartoon characters immortalized in the cookie jar hall of fame.*

mixer, beat in the egg whites until well mixed, then increase the speed and continue beating until the whites are stiff. If you like, divide the icing into small bowls and add a few drops of food coloring to each portion. Add a little lemon juice or rum to achieve a spreading consistency. Spoon the icing into one or more paper cones (see page 81), and pipe decorations onto the cookies. Allow to dry for 2 hours at room temperature. Store in airtight containers.

Molded
cookies

Almond and Ginger Biscotti

Delicious with espresso coffee or dipped in sweet Italian wine—Vin Santo—these dry, crunchy cookies are an Italian version of German almond bread. **Makes about 4 dozen cookies**

2½ cups all-purpose flour

½ cup ground almonds

1 teaspoon baking soda

½ teaspoon salt

½ teaspoon allspice

1 teaspoon ground ginger

1½ cups blanched almonds, toasted and coarsely chopped

¾ cup pine nuts, toasted

2 eggs

1 cup superfine sugar

½ cup packed light brown sugar

¼ cup (½ stick) unsalted butter, melted and cooled

1½ teaspoons almond or vanilla extract

Grated zest of 1 lemon

2 tablespoons (1 ounce) chopped, candied ginger

Milk, for glazing

1. Preheat the oven to 375°F. Line a large baking sheet with heavy-duty aluminum foil. In a large bowl, combine the flour, ground almonds, baking soda, salt, allspice, ground ginger, chopped almonds, and pine nuts.

2. In another bowl, whisk the eggs until foamy, then whisk in the sugars, melted butter, almond or vanilla extract, lemon zest,

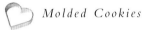

and candied ginger. Gradually stir the flour mixture into the egg mixture until a dough forms.

3. Turn out onto a lightly floured surface and knead lightly, just until the nuts are evenly distributed through the dough. Divide the dough in half and form into two log shapes about 3 inches wide and 10 inches long.

4. Using a thin-bladed metal spatula, transfer each log to the baking sheet, placing them 2–3 inches apart. Lightly brush each log with a little milk and bake for about 25 minutes, rotating the baking sheet from front to back halfway through the cooking time to bake evenly. The logs are cooked when golden and a toothpick inserted into the center comes out clean. Remove the baking sheet to a wire rack to cool for about 10 minutes. Reduce the oven temperature to 325°F.

5. While the logs are still warm and soft, use a sharp knife to score each log crosswise into ½-inch slices. Transfer to a work surface and allow to cool for another 5 minutes. Using a sharp, serrated knife, carefully cut through the scored slices and arrange, cut sides down, on a baking sheet (you may need another large baking sheet at this point).

6. Bake the biscotti for about 20 minutes, until golden and crisp, turning once halfway through the cooking time to bake evenly. Remove the biscotti to wire racks to cool completely. Allow the biscotti to stand for 2–3 hours, until crisp, then store in airtight containers or jars.

TIP

○ **Candied ginger is available in some large supermarkets and specialty stores.**

Pine Nut Macaroons

These delicious cookies are full of almond and pine nut flavors. Try making a sandwich cookie using a little apricot jam, as they do in Italy. **Makes about 2 dozen cookies**

3 tablespoons currants
3 tablespoons Marsala or
   sweet wine
¾ cup slivered blanched
   almonds, lightly toasted
½ cup pine nuts, toasted
½ cup superfine sugar
1 tablespoon all-purpose
   flour
1 egg white

¼ teaspoon almond
   extract
1 cup pine nuts

RIGHT: *This Umbrella Kids cookie jar was made by American Bisque, which produced jars for over forty years.*

1. Preheat the oven to 350°F. Line a large baking sheet with foil (shiny side up) or nonstick baking parchment. In a small bowl, combine the currants and Marsala or sweet wine, and heat in a microwave oven on high for 30–60 seconds. Allow to stand 3–5 minutes, until the liquid is absorbed, then cool.

2. In a food processor, using a metal blade, process the toasted almonds and pine nuts,

sugar, and flour until finely ground. Add the egg white and almond extract and, using the pulse button, process until the mixture forms a dough. Turn the dough into a bowl and stir in the currants.

3. Put the untoasted pine nuts into a medium bowl or pie tray. Wet your hands and, using a teaspoon to scoop out the dough, shape it into ¾-inch balls. Roll the balls in the pine nuts, pressing lightly to cover completely. Place the balls 1½ inches apart on the baking sheet. Flatten slightly to make a disk shape.

4. Bake the cookies for 12–15 minutes, until the pine nuts are golden, rotating the baking sheet from front to back halfway through cooking. Remove to a wire rack to cool for 2–3 minutes. Remove the cookies to a wire rack to cool completely. Store in an airtight container.

Peanut Butter Cookie Cups

The combination of chocolate and peanut butter is a popular one. This peanutty cookie, filled with a creamy chocolate ganache swirl, is heavenly! **Makes about 2 dozen cookies**

1 cup all-purpose flour
1 teaspoon baking powder
1/4 teaspoon salt
1/2 cup (1 stick) unsalted butter, softened
1/2 cup packed light brown sugar
1/4 cup sugar
1 cup smooth peanut butter

1 egg
1 teaspoon vanilla extract

CHOCOLATE FILLING
12 oz. semisweet chocolate, chopped
6 tablespoons (3/4 stick) unsalted butter, softened

1. Sift the flour, baking powder, and salt in a small bowl. In a large mixing bowl, using an electric mixer, beat the butter for 1 minute, until creamy. Add the sugars and continue beating until the mixture is light and fluffy. Add the peanut butter in three batches, beating well after each addition, until the mixture is well blended. Beat in the egg and vanilla extract. Stir in the flour mixture until just blended. Refrigerate the dough for about 1 hour, until chilled.

2. Preheat the oven to 375°F. Scoop out tablespoons of the mixture and, using slightly moistened hands, roll between your palms to form 1-inch balls. Place the balls 1½ inches apart on two large, ungreased baking sheets. Using the handle of a wooden spoon, press down into the center of each ball to make a deep hole. Bake 10–12 minutes, until just set and golden, rotating the sheets between the top and bottom shelves, and from front to back, halfway through the cooking time.

3. Remove the baking sheets to wire racks to cool for 2–3 minutes, until the cookies are firm enough to move. Using a metal spatula, transfer to a wire rack to cool. Repeat with the remaining mixture.

4. When the cookies are completely cooled, put the chocolate into a medium bowl. Set the bowl over a saucepan of barely simmering water and heat until the chocolate is melted and smooth, stirring frequently. Remove from the heat and cool slightly.

5. Gently beat in the butter until the mixture just thickens. Allow to cool slightly, then spoon into a decorating bag fitted with a medium star tip. Pipe a small amount of chocolate ganache into the center of each cookie and allow to set until firm. Store in airtight containers, with waxed paper between the layers.

Right: *The Brush Teddy Bear is just one of a number of cookie jar designs inspired by furry creatures.*

Cinnamon Cookies

These contain no flour, and are similar to the cinnamon balls traditionally served at Passover.

Makes about 20 cookies

2 cups finely blanched
  almonds, walnuts, or
  pecans
1 cup superfine sugar
1 tablespoon ground
  cinnamon
2 egg whites
1/8 teaspoon cream
  of tartar

FOR DUSTING
1 tablespoon
  confectioners' sugar
1 teaspoon ground
  cinnamon

RIGHT: *The Collegiate Owl was made in a variety of colors, this one being the most appealing.*

1. Preheat the oven to 325°F. Lightly grease a large, nonstick baking sheet. In a medium bowl, combine the ground nuts, ½ cup sugar, and the cinnamon.

2. In a medium bowl, using an electric mixer, beat the egg whites until foamy. Add the cream of tartar and continue beating until soft peaks form. Gradually add the remaining

LEFT: *The cat's tail provides a convenient handle for American Bisque's Cat on a Box cookie jar.*

172

sugar, a tablespoon at a time, beating well after each addition, until the whites are stiff and glossy. Gently fold in the nut mixture.

3. With moistened hands, shape the mixture into 2-inch balls and flatten slightly. Place on the baking sheets 1 inch apart. Bake for about 25 minutes, until set and golden, rotating the sheets between the top and bottom shelves, and from front to back, halfway through the cooking time.

4. Remove the baking sheets to wire racks to cool. Dust the cookies with confectioners' sugar, then sprinkle with the cinnamon. Store in an airtight container.

VARIATION

○ **Shape the dough into walnut-size balls and roll in a sugar and cinnamon mixture to coat completely. You will need 1/2 cup of confectioners' sugar and 1 tablespoon of cinnamon.**

Chocolate Pretzels

These chocolate pretzels are surprisingly easy to form—just be sure to chill the dough long enough. **Makes about 20 cookies**

1 cup all-purpose flour
¼ teaspoon salt
3 tablespoons unsweetened cocoa powder
½ cup (1 stick) unsalted butter, softened
⅔ cup superfine sugar
1 egg, lightly beaten
1 teaspoon vanilla extract

GLAZE
1 egg white, lightly beaten
Sugar crystals, for sprinkling

1. Lightly grease two large baking sheets. In a medium bowl, sift together the flour, salt, and cocoa powder.

2. In a large bowl, beat the butter for about 1 minute, until creamy. Add the sugar and continue beating for 1–2 minutes, until light and fluffy. Beat in the egg and vanilla extract, until well blended.

3. On low speed, gradually add the flour mixture until a soft dough forms. Turn the dough onto a piece of plastic wrap. Shape into a ball, flatten to a disk shape, and wrap tightly. Refrigerate until firm, about 1 hour.

4. Preheat the oven to 375°F. With lightly floured hands, roll tablespoonfuls of the dough into about twenty 1½-inch balls. On a lightly floured surface, roll each dough ball into a "rope" about 10–12 inches long. Holding each end of the rope with the fingers, bring the ends together to the center of the rope. Twist the ends together and press into the middle of the rope to form a pretzel shape. Transfer the pretzels to the prepared baking sheets.

5. Brush each pretzel with a little egg white to glaze, then sprinkle with the sugar crystals. Bake for about 10 minutes, until the pretzels feel firm to the fingertips. Remove the baking sheets to wire racks and cool slightly until the pretzels are firm enough to move. Using a metal spatula, transfer the cookies to wire racks to cool completely. Store in airtight containers.

Chocolate-Dipped Hazelnut Crescents

Austrian crescents are generally made with ground almonds. This variety uses hazelnuts, which go beautifully with chocolate. **Makes about 3 dozen cookies**

1 cup all-purpose flour
1 cup cake flour
1/4 teaspoon salt
2/3 cup hazelnuts,
  toasted until golden
1 cup (2 sticks) unsalted
  butter, softened
1/3 cup superfine sugar
1 tablespoon hazelnut
  or almond liqueur

1 teaspoon vanilla
  extract
Confectioners' sugar,
  for dusting
6 oz. semisweet
  chocolate, melted

RIGHT: *American Bisque's Jack-in-the-Box cookie jar.*

1. Sift the flours and salt into a medium bowl and stir to mix well.

2. Preheat the oven to 325°F. In a food processor, using a metal blade, process the toasted hazelnuts until fine crumbs form; the nuts should be finely chopped but not ground.

3. In a large bowl, using an electric mixer, beat the butter for about 1 minute, until creamy. Add the sugar and beat for 1–2 minutes, until the mixture is light and fluffy. Beat in the liqueur and vanilla extract. Gently stir in the flour mixture until just blended, then fold in the finely chopped hazelnuts.

4. With lightly floured hands, form the dough into 1½-inch balls, placing them on a large baking sheet until all the dough is used. Roll each ball into a 2 x ½-inch crescent shape, and place 2 inches apart on another large, ungreased baking sheet. Bake for 20–25 minutes, until the edges are set and the cookies are lightly golden, rotating the baking sheet from front to back halfway through the cooking time. Remove the baking sheet to a wire rack to cool for 10 minutes. Remove each cookie to a wire rack to cool completely. Repeat with the remaining crescents until they are all baked.

5. Arrange the crescents side by side on a wire rack set over a baking sheet to catch drips, then dust them with plenty of confectioners' sugar. Using kitchen tongs or fingers, dip half of each cookie into the melted chocolate, or spoon a "strip" of chocolate over the center. Place the crescents on waxed paper–lined baking sheets and refrigerate for 10–15 minutes, until set. Store in an airtight container, with waxed paper between the layers.

German Pepper Nuts

*These peppery, sugar-coated cookies are popular all over Northern Europe and
Scandinavia at Christmastime.* **Makes about 40 cookies**

3 1/2 cups all-purpose
  flour
3/4 teaspoon baking soda
3/4 teaspoon baking
  powder
3/4 teaspoon salt
1 teaspoon ground
  cinnamon
1/2 teaspoon ground
  white pepper

1/2 teaspoon ground
  ginger
1/4 teaspoon ground
  cloves
3 tablespoons
  vegetable shortening
1 cup honey
1 egg
Confectioners' sugar,
  for dusting

1. Sift the flour, baking soda, baking powder,
salt, cinnamon, white pepper, ginger, and
cloves into a large bowl and stir well to mix.
2. In another large bowl, beat the shortening
for about 1 minute, until creamy. Gradually
add the honey and continue beating until
well blended, scraping the bowl occasionally.
Beat in the egg. With the mixer on low
speed, gradually beat in the flour mixture for
2–3 minutes, until a soft dough forms. Shape

the dough into a ball and flatten slightly to a disk shape, wrap tightly in plastic wrap, and refrigerate for 1–2 hours until firm.

3. Preheat the oven to 350°F. Lightly grease two large baking sheets. Knead the dough to soften slightly. Pull off small pieces of dough and, using floured hands, roll into 1-inch balls. Place balls 1 inch apart on the baking sheets.

4. Bake for about 15 minutes, until golden and slightly cracked, rotating baking sheets between the top and bottom shelves, and from front to back, halfway through the cooking time. Remove baking sheets to wire racks to cool slightly. Using a spatula, remove the cookies to wire racks to cool completely. Repeat with the remaining cookie dough.

5. When cool, place the confectioners' sugar in a small bowl, drop each cookie into the sugar, and roll to coat well. Store the cookies in airtight containers.

Peppermint Cookie Canes

This basic cookie dough is tinted with food coloring before being formed into candy cane shapes. Tie with a ribbon and use as Christmas decorations. **Makes about 2 dozen**

2 1/2 cups all-purpose
  flour
1/4 teaspoon salt
1 cup (2 sticks) unsalted
  butter, softened
1 cup confectioners'
  sugar, sifted
1 egg, lightly beaten
1/2 teaspoon vanilla
  extract

1/2 teaspoon peppermint
  extract
1/4 teaspoon red food
  coloring (optional)
1/4 cup crushed
  peppermint candy

RIGHT: *The Kittens and Yarn cookie jar is another American Bisque design.*

Please turn over.

1. Sift the flour and salt in a medium bowl. In a large bowl, using an electric mixer, beat the butter for about 30 seconds, until creamy. Gradually add the sugar and beat for 1–2 minutes, until light and fluffy. Beat in the egg and the vanilla and peppermint extracts, until blended. With the mixer on low speed, gradually beat in the flour.

2. Remove half the dough and wrap tightly in a piece of plastic wrap. Add the red food coloring and crushed peppermint candy to the remaining dough and beat until thoroughly mixed. Wrap tightly in plastic wrap and refrigerate both doughs for about 1 hour, until firm.

3. Preheat the oven to 350°F. Line two large baking sheets with aluminum foil or nonstick baking parchment. To form the cookies, use a teaspoon to scoop a piece of plain dough, then roll into a rope shape 4–6 inches long. Repeat with the red-colored dough, then gently twist the two ropes together and bend the top end to make a cane shape. Repeat with the remaining doughs and set the canes about 2 inches apart on the baking sheets.

4. Bake the canes for 8–10 minutes, until firm; do not allow them to brown or the color effect will be lost. Remove the baking sheets to wire racks to cool slightly for a few minutes. Transfer the canes to wire racks to cool completely. Store in airtight containers.

CLOCKWISE FROM RIGHT:
Cookie Jar Gingersnaps,
Mexican Wedding
Cakes, and Honey
and Lemon
Madeleines

Cookie Jar Gingersnaps

A classic cookie jar favorite with adults, gingersnaps combine sugar, spices, and molasses to great effect. **Makes about 4 dozen cookies**

2 cups all-purpose flour
1 tablespoon ground
  ginger
2 teaspoons baking soda
1 1/2 teaspoons ground
  cinnamon
1/2 teaspoon ground
  cloves
1/2 teaspoon salt
3/4 cup vegetable
  shortening

1 cup sugar
1 egg, lightly beaten
1/4 cup molasses
Sugar, for rolling

VAN HOUTEN'S COCOA.

VAN HOUTEN'S COCOA

Please turn over

1. Preheat the oven to 350°F. Sift the flour, ginger, baking soda, cinnamon, ground cloves, and salt in a medium bowl.

2. In a large bowl, using an electric mixer, beat the shortening for 1 minute, until soft. Gradually add the sugar and continue beating until the mixture is light and fluffy. Beat in the egg and molasses, then stir in the flour mixture until thoroughly blended.

3. Pour the sugar into a medium bowl. Scoop out heaping teaspoons of the cookie

mixture and, using your palms, roll into
3/4-inch balls, then roll in the sugar. Place
2 inches apart on ungreased baking sheets.

4. Bake for about 10 minutes, until the tops
are lightly browned and crackled. Remove
the baking sheets to wire racks to cool.
Remove the cookies to wire racks to cool
completely. Store in an airtight container.

RIGHT: *The Humpty Dumpty jar, made by Purinton,
is inspired by the famous nursery rhyme.*

Honey and Lemon Madeleines

Using madeleine molds allows you to make pretty and delicate-looking cookies.

Makes about 1 dozen cookies

1 cup plus 1 tablespoon
   all-purpose flour, sifted
1 teaspoon baking
   powder
Butter, for greasing
2 eggs
1/3 cup honey
1/4 cup superfine sugar
Grated zest of 1 lemon
1 tablespoon lemon juice

1/2 teaspoon vanilla
   extract
6 tablespoons (3/4 stick)
   unsalted butter, melted
Confectioners'
sugar, for
dusting

1. Preheat the oven to 375°F. Sift the
flour and baking powder into a small bowl.
Lightly butter a 12-cup madeleine mold.
In a large bowl, using an electric mixer, beat
the eggs, honey, and sugar for 5–7 minutes,
until light and pale and a slowly falling
ribbon forms when the beaters are lifted
from the bowl. Gently fold in the
lemon zest and juice and the
vanilla extract.

2. Beginning and ending with the flour, alternately fold in the flour and cooled melted butter in four or five batches. Allow the batter to rest for 10 minutes, then spoon into the molds, almost filling them.

3. Bake for 10–12 minutes, until the tops spring back when gently pressed, rotating the molds from front to back after 8 minutes. Unmold onto a wire rack to cool. Dust with confectioners' sugar.

Mexican Wedding Cakes

Mexican wedding cakes are a traditional cookie, so called because they resemble wedding bells, thickly dusted with confectioners' sugar. **Makes about 3 dozen cookies**

¾ cup pecan halves

¾ cup confectioners' sugar

½ teaspoon ground cinnamon

1 cup (2 sticks) butter, cubed and softened

1 teaspoon vanilla extract

2 cups all-purpose flour

¼ teaspoon salt

Confectioners' sugar, for rolling

1. Preheat the oven to 375°F. Put the pecans on a baking sheet and toast for 7–10 minutes, until golden, stirring and shaking the baking sheet occasionally. Pour onto a plate to cool completely. Turn off the oven.

2. In a food processor, using a metal blade, process the pecans with the confectioners' sugar and cinnamon until fine crumbs form. Add the butter and process until creamy and smooth, scraping the side of the bowl once. Add the vanilla extract and pulse to blend.

Add the flour and salt and, using the pulse action, process until the mixture begins to stick together and form a soft dough. Scrape into a bowl, cover, and refrigerate for 1–2 hours, until firm.

3. Preheat the oven to 375°F. With lightly floured hands, shape the dough piece by piece into 1-inch balls. Place the balls 1½ inches apart on two large, ungreased baking sheets. Bake for about 10 minutes, until the cookies are barely golden, rotating the baking sheets from the top to the bottom shelf and from front to back halfway through the cooking time. Remove the baking sheets to wire racks to cool for 2 minutes.

4. Put about 1 cup of confectioners' sugar into a medium bowl. While the cookies are still warm, drop them into the bowl, a few at a time, and roll to coat well. Transfer to wire racks to cool completely. Repeat with the remaining dough. Roll again in confectioners' sugar and store in airtight containers.

Chocolate, Orange, and Hazelnut Biscotti

In this biscotti recipe, a chocolate dough is scented with orange and studded with hazelnuts and chocolate chips for a rich result. **Makes about 3 dozen**

2 cups all-purpose flour

1 1/2 teaspoons baking powder

1 teaspoon salt

3/4 teaspoon ground cinnamon

1/2 teaspoon ground ginger

1/2 cup (1 stick) unsalted butter, softened

1 1/4 cups superfine sugar

2 eggs, lightly beaten

Grated zest of 1 orange

1/4 cup freshly squeezed orange juice

1 3/4 cups hazelnuts, toasted, husked, and coarsely chopped

1 cup semisweet chocolate chips

1 lb. semisweet chocolate, melted

1. In a large bowl, combine the flour, baking powder, salt, ground cinnamon, and ginger. In another large bowl, using an electric mixer, beat the butter for about 1 minute, until creamy. Add the sugar and beat for 1–2 minutes, until light and fluffy. On low speed, slowly add the eggs, orange zest, and juice; increase the speed to medium and beat until well blended. On low speed, gradually add the flour mixture until a soft dough forms. Add the nuts and chocolate chips, and

stir to distribute evenly. Form the dough into a rough ball.

2. Divide the dough in half. Lay two pieces of plastic wrap or foil on a work surface and place one dough half on each piece. Using the plastic wrap or foil as a guide, form each dough half into a log shape about 3 inches in diameter. Wrap tightly and refrigerate for 20–30 minutes, until firm.

3. Preheat the oven to 375°F. Line a large baking sheet with heavy-duty aluminum foil. Place the dough logs 3–4 inches apart on the baking sheet and flatten the logs slightly to an oval shape. Bake for about 25 minutes, until golden brown, the tops begin to crack, and a toothpick inserted into the center of the log comes out clean. Rotate the baking sheet from front to back, halfway through the cooking time, to ensure even baking. Remove the baking sheet to a wire rack to cool for about 10 minutes. Reduce the oven temperature to 325°F.

4. While the logs are still warm and soft, score them crosswise into 1/4–1/2-inch slices using a sharp knife. Slide the foil onto the work surface and allow the logs to cool for about 10 minutes, until beginning to firm. Using a sharp, serrated knife, cut through the scored slices and arrange the cut slices on the baking sheet (you may need another large baking sheet at this point). Bake the biscotti for 25–30 minutes, until golden and crisp, turning once halfway through the cooking time. Remove the biscotti to wire racks to cool completely. Allow the biscotti to stand for 2–3 hours, until crisp.

5. Line a large baking sheet with waxed paper. Place the melted chocolate in a bowl and dip each biscotti halfway into it. Place the biscotti on the waxed paper–lined baking sheets for 15–20 minutes to set. Store in the refrigerator or in an airtight container, with waxed paper between layers.

Spice Cookies

These crunchy, wholesome cookies are delicious with coffee or tea.

Makes about 15 cookies

1 cup whole-wheat flour

1/2 teaspoon baking soda

1 teaspoon ground
   cinnamon

1 teaspoon allspice

1/2 cup quick-cooking oats

1/2 cup packed light
   brown sugar

6 tablespoons butter

1 tablespoon corn syrup

1 tablespoon milk

1. Preheat the oven to 350°F. Lightly grease two large baking sheets. Sift the flour, baking soda, cinnamon, and allspice in a large bowl. Stir in the oats and sugar until blended.

2. In a small saucepan, melt the butter with the corn syrup and milk. Make a well in the center of the flour mixture, pour in the butter mixture, and beat until a smooth,

pliable dough forms. Divide the dough into fifteen small balls and place 3 inches apart on the baking sheets. Flatten each ball slightly with the back of a wet spoon.

3. Bake for about 15 minutes, until golden brown. Remove the baking sheets to wire racks to cool slightly. Transfer the cookies to wire racks to cool completely. Store in airtight containers.

Snickerdoodles

These traditional New England cookies also go by the name of "snipdoodles."

Makes about 4 dozen cookies

3 ½ cups all-purpose
  flour
1 teaspoon baking soda
1 teaspoon ground
  cinnamon
½ teaspoon ground
  nutmeg
½ cup (1 stick) unsalted
  butter, softened
1⅓ cups sugar
2 eggs

¼ cup milk
1 teaspoon vanilla
  extract
½ cup chopped walnuts
½ cup currants
½ cup sugar
2 tablespoons ground
  cinnamon
1 teaspoon ground
  nutmeg

1. Lightly grease two large baking sheets. In a large bowl, sift together the flour, baking soda, ground cinnamon, and nutmeg. Set aside.

2. In a large bowl, beat the butter for about 1 minute, until creamy. Add the sugar and beat for 1–2 minutes, until light and fluffy. Beat in the eggs, one at a time, then slowly beat in the milk and vanilla extract until well blended. Stir in the flour until blended, then the chopped nuts and currants. Refrigerate the dough for 15–20 minutes, until just firm.

3. Preheat the oven to 375°F. Mix the sugar, cinnamon, and nutmeg in a small bowl. Roll tablespoonfuls of dough into 1½-inch balls, then roll in the sugar and spice mixture. Place the balls 2 inches apart on the baking sheets, flatten slightly, and bake for 10 minutes, until golden. Remove cookies to wire racks to cool completely. Store in airtight containers.

RIGHT: *This advertisement jar for Nestlé's Toll House cookies is now a highly collectible item.*

Chinese Almond Cookies

These cookies make an unusual but delicious addition to the cookie jar.

Makes about 30 cookies

1 cup all-purpose flour
1 teaspoon baking powder
1/4 teaspoon salt
1/2 cup (1 stick) unsalted butter, softened
1/4 cup sugar
2 tablespoons light brown sugar
1 egg, beaten

1/2 teaspoon almond extract
1/4 cup ground almonds
2 tablespoons water
30 whole blanched almonds

1. Preheat the oven to 350°F. Lightly grease two large baking sheets. Sift the flour, baking powder, and salt in a bowl. In a medium bowl, using an electric mixer, beat the butter and sugars together, until light and fluffy.

2. Add half the beaten egg and the almond extract to the butter and sugar mixture and beat until smooth. Stir in the flour mixture, then the ground almonds, until blended.

3. Shape the mixture into small balls and arrange 2–3 inches apart on the baking

sheets. Flatten the cookies slightly and press an almond into the center of each one. Beat the remaining egg with the water and brush over the tops of the cookies. Bake for 12–15 minutes, until pale golden. Remove the sheets to wire racks to cool slightly, then transfer the cookies to wire racks to cool completely.

LEFT: *Popeye's enemy, Bluto, is the subject of this wonderfully wacky jar, made in the 1980s.*

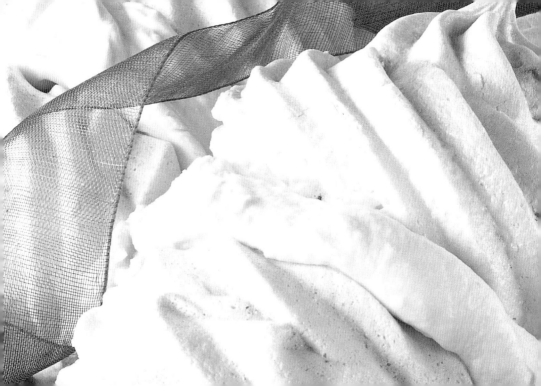

Pressed & Piped

cookies

Chocolate Amaretti

Surprisingly easy to make, these chocolate-almond cookies resemble a rich, chewy macaroon. Be sure the dough is firm enough to pipe.

Makes about 2 dozen cookies

1 cup blanched whole
  almonds

$^1/_2$ cup superfine sugar

1 tablespoon
  unsweetened cocoa
  powder (preferably
  Dutch-processed)

2 tablespoons
  confectioners' sugar

2 medium egg whites

$^1/_8$ teaspoon cream
  of tartar

$^1/_2$ teaspoon vanilla
  extract

$^1/_2$ teaspoon almond
  extract

Slivered almonds,
  to decorate (optional)

1. Preheat the oven to 350°F. Spread the blanched almonds on a small baking sheet and toast for 7–10 minutes, until golden and fragrant. Pour onto a plate to cool completely. Reduce the oven temperature to 325°F. Line a large baking sheet with nonstick baking parchment or lightly greased foil.

2. Put the toasted almonds and 2 tablespoons of superfine sugar into the bowl of a food processor. Using the metal blade, process until finely ground but not oily. Add the cocoa powder and confectioners' sugar and, using the pulse action, process to blend well.

3. In a medium bowl, beat the egg whites until foamy. Add the cream of tartar and continue beating until stiff peaks form. Sprinkle in the remaining superfine sugar, a tablespoon at a time, beating well after each addition, until the whites are stiff and glossy. Beat in the vanilla and almond extracts, then gently fold in the almond-cocoa mixture until just blended.

4. Spoon the mixture into a large pastry bag fitted with a plain ½-inch tip. Pipe 1½-inch mounds 1 inch apart onto the baking sheet. If you like, sprinkle a few slivered almonds onto the center of each mound.

5. Bake for 10–12 minutes, until the cookies are firm on top and the surface is slightly crisp. Remove the baking sheet to a wire rack to cool slightly. Using a spatula, remove the cookies to a wire rack to cool completely. Store in an airtight container.

Old-Fashioned Butter Cookies

*These Danish cookies use real vanilla seeds from a bean, but you can use vanilla extract,
although they won't be quite as authentic.* **Makes about 2 dozen cookies**

1 3/4 cups all-purpose
flour

2 tablespoons cornstarch

5 tablespoons sugar

1/3 cup blanched almonds,
finely chopped

1/2 vanilla bean or
1 teaspoon vanilla
extract

1 cup unsalted butter,
cut into small pieces

1 egg, separated

Sugar, for sprinkling

Confectioners' sugar,
for dusting

Butter

1. Preheat the oven to 400°F. Lightly grease two large baking sheets. In a large bowl, sift together the flour and cornstarch. Stir in the sugar and chopped almonds.

2. With a sharp knife, split the vanilla bean and scrape out the seeds. Add to the flour mixture and mix well. (If using vanilla extract, mix with the egg yolk.)

LEFT: *The Secrets cookie jar, made by the A. Little Company, has a highly original design.*

3. With a pastry blender or electric mixer on slow speed, cut in the butter until fine crumbs form. In a small bowl, beat the egg yolk (and vanilla extract, if using). Add to the flour-butter mixture and knead until a soft but firm dough forms. (If the dough is very sticky, sprinkle with a little more flour.)

4. Spoon the dough into a large pastry bag fitted with a large plain tip and pipe 2-inch rings, 1½ inches apart, onto the baking sheets. In a small bowl, beat the egg white until foamy and lightly brush each ring. Sprinkle with the sugar.

5. Bake for about 8 minutes, until lightly golden and set. Remove baking sheets to wire racks to cool slightly. Using a metal spatula, remove the cookies to wire racks to cool completely. Dust with confectioners' sugar. Store in an airtight container.

Chocolate Viennese Fingers

This delicious, butter-rich cookie comes from Austria.

Makes about 2 dozen cookies

*Vegetable oil spray
    or vegetable oil,
    for greasing
2 cups all-purpose flour
⅓ cup unsweetened
    cocoa powder
¼ cup cornstarch
1 cup (2 sticks) unsalted
    butter, softened
½ cup confectioners'
    sugar, sifted*

*1 teaspoon vanilla
    extract
Confectioners' sugar,
    for dusting
4 oz. bittersweet or
    semisweet chocolate,
    melted (optional)*

RIGHT: *This American
Bisque Donald Duck jar
dates from the 1950s.*

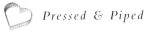

1. Preheat the oven to 350°F. Lightly spray or grease two large baking sheets. Sift the flour, cocoa powder, and cornstarch into a medium bowl.

2. In a large bowl, using an electric mixer, beat the butter and confectioners' sugar for 1–2 minutes, until light and fluffy. On low speed, gradually beat in the flour mixture and vanilla extract until a soft dough forms.

3. Spoon the dough into a large pastry bag fitted with a large star tip. Pipe about twenty-four 3-inch fingers or *S*-shapes 2 inches apart on the baking sheets.

4. Bake for 15–20 minutes, until set and slightly firm when touched with a fingertip, rotating the baking sheets between the top and bottom shelves, and from front to back, halfway through the cooking time. Remove the baking sheets to wire racks to cool for about 15 minutes, until the cookies are firm. Using a spatula, transfer the cookies to wire racks to cool completely.

5. Arrange the cookies close together on a wire rack and dust with confectioners' sugar. Drizzle with the melted chocolate, or dip one end of each cookie halfway into the chocolate and tap off any excess. Place the cookies on a waxed paper–lined baking sheet and allow to set. Store in airtight containers, with waxed paper between the layers.

Spiral Spice Cookies

Spice-cookie doughs were popular in New England and the Pennsylvania Dutch country, especially in the autumn. Look for whole nutmegs. **Makes about 12 cookies**

1½ cups all-purpose
   flour
½ teaspoon baking
   soda
1 teaspoon ground
   cinnamon
½ teaspoon freshly
   grated nutmeg
½ teaspoon ground
   ginger

½ teaspoon ground
   cardamom
¼ teaspoon finely
   ground black pepper
⅛ teaspoon salt
⅓ cup vegetable
   shortening
⅓ cup sugar
⅓ cup molasses
1 egg

2 tablespoons cider
   vinegar
Vegetable oil spray
   or vegetable oil,
   for greasing
Confectioners' sugar,
   for dusting

1. Sift the flour, baking soda, cinnamon, nutmeg, ginger, cardamom, black pepper, and salt in a medium bowl.

2. In a large bowl, using an electric mixer, beat the shortening and sugar for 1–2 minutes, until light and fluffy. Beat in the molasses, egg, and vinegar until well blended. On low speed, beat in the flour

LEFT: *Cinderella's pumpkin coach and mice coachmen are the inspiration for this charming jar.*

and spice mixture until a soft dough forms.

3. Preheat the oven to 350°F. Lightly spray or grease two large baking sheets. Spoon the dough into a large pastry bag fitted with a ¼-inch plain tip. Pipe the dough into 3-inch circles, beginning at the center point and working to the outer edge, 2 inches apart on the baking sheets.

4. Bake for about 10 minutes, until the cookies are just set and beginning to brown around the edges. Remove the baking sheets to wire racks to cool slightly. Using a metal spatula, transfer the cookies to wire racks to cool completely. Lightly dust the cookies with confectioners' sugar. Store in airtight containers.

Almond-Meringue Cream Sandwiches

Classic meringues sandwiched with whipped cream are one of the favorite fancy cookies for special occasions.

Makes about 14 sandwiches or 28 meringues

4 egg whites

1/8 teaspoon cream
of tartar

1 1/4 cups superfine sugar

1/2 teaspoon almond
extract

1 cup blanched almonds,
toasted and chopped

1 cup heavy or
whipping cream

1−2 tablespoons
Amaretto liqueur,
to serve

RIGHT: *Popeye is a popular character jar. This is a 1980s reproduction of an original American Bisque cookie jar.*

1. Preheat the oven to 200°F. Line two large baking sheets with foil or nonstick baking parchment.

2. In a large bowl, using an electric mixer, beat the egg whites until foamy. Add the cream of tartar and continue beating on high speed until stiff peaks form. Gradually add the sugar a tablespoon at a time, beating well after each addition, until the whites are stiff and glossy. Beat in the almond extract and gently fold in the chopped almonds.

3. Gently spoon the mixture into a large pastry bag fitted with a large star tip. Pipe an even number of 1½–2-inch rosettes about 1½ inches apart onto the prepared baking sheets.

4. Bake the meringues for about 1 hour, until set and cooked through, rotating the baking sheets between the top and bottom shelves, and from front to back, halfway through the cooking time. Do not allow the meringues to brown. Turn off the oven but do not remove the meringues; allow them to stay in the oven for another hour. Remove the baking sheets from the oven and peel the meringues off the foil or paper. Arrange on wire racks to cool completely. Store unfilled meringues in airtight containers.

5. To serve, whip the cream and Amaretto in a medium bowl until soft peaks form. Spread a little cream on one meringue and sandwich with another. Continue with the remaining meringues and cream.

Chocolate Cherry Spritz

These rich chocolate spritz cookies are usually pressed through a cookie press but they can also be piped. **Makes about 4¹/₂ dozen**

2 oz. unsweetened
  chocolate, chopped
¹/₂ cup unsalted butter,
  softened
1 cup superfine sugar
¹/₄ teaspoon salt
1 egg
1 teaspoon vanilla
  extract

2 tablespoons milk
2 cups all-purpose
  flour, sifted
Candied cherries,
  cut in half

1. Preheat the oven to 350°F. Place the chocolate in a medium bowl and set over a saucepan of barely simmering water. Heat over low heat until melted and smooth, stirring frequently. Remove from the heat and set aside to cool.

2. In a large bowl, using an electric mixer, beat the butter for about 1 minute, until creamy. Add the sugar and salt and continue beating for 1–2 minutes, until light and fluffy. Beat in the egg, vanilla extract, and milk until blended, then beat in the cooled melted chocolate until well blended. On low speed, beat in the flour until a soft dough forms. Add a little flour if the dough is too soft.

3. Pack the dough into a cookie press fitted with the design plate of your choice. Press out the dough 1½ inches apart onto two cold, ungreased baking sheets. Press a cherry half into the center of each cookie and bake 8–10 minutes, until slightly puffed and crisp. Remove baking sheets to wire racks and,

before cookies cool and crisp, transfer them to wire racks to cool completely. Repeat with the remaining dough. Store the cookies in airtight containers.

TIP

○ **This cookie dough can be spooned into a large pastry bag fitted with a large star tip. Pipe 2-inch rosettes, arrange, and bake as above.**

Spritz Cookies

Spritz cookies are a tender, rich butter cookie made with a cookie press. A variety of design plates produce several different shapes, but the dough must be just the right consistency.

Makes about 4¹/₂ dozen cookies

FAR LEFT:
Spritz Cookies
LEFT: *Strawberry*
Thumbprints

1 cup (2 sticks) unsalted
  butter, softened
¹/₂ cup superfine sugar
1 egg, lightly beaten
1¹/₂ teaspoons vanilla
  extract
2–2¹/₂ cups all-purpose
  flour, sifted
Sugar sprinkles, to
  decorate

1. Preheat the oven to 375°F. In a large bowl, using an electric mixer, beat the butter for 30–60 seconds, until creamy. Add the sugar and continue beating for 1–2 minutes, until the mixture is light and fluffy. Beat in the egg and vanilla extract.

2. On low speed, gradually beat in about 2¹/₄ cups of flour until a soft dough forms. If the dough is too soft, add a little more flour until it reaches a manageable consistency.★

3. Pack the cookie dough into a cookie press fitted with the design plate of your choice. Press out the cookies onto two cold, ungreased baking sheets. Depending on the shape, sprinkle each cookie with a few sprinkles or other cookie decorations, or press a candied cherry into the center of each cookie.

4. Bake for about 8 minutes, until set and just golden. Remove the baking sheets to wire racks to cool slightly. Using a thin-bladed metal spatula, transfer the cookies to wire racks to cool completely. Repeat with the remaining cookie dough. Store the cookies in airtight containers.

★ Cookie press cookies can be difficult to form unless the dough is the right temperature. If the dough or weather is too warm, the dough won't hold its shape and may have to be chilled for about 30 minutes before pressing. If the dough is chilled too long or is too firm, it will be difficult to press through the design plate. To stiffen the dough, add a little more flour. If it is too stiff, add a little milk. Form a log shape slightly smaller than the diameter of the cookie press and insert into the prepared press. Every cookie press has its own directions, which you should read thoroughly. You may want to practice a few times.

LEFT: *The Educated Tree is a rare cookie jar produced by the Metlox Company of Manhattan Beach, California.*

235

Strawberry Thumbprints

Pressing a thumb into each cookie mound gives these classic cookies their name. For a fancier cookie, the dough can be piped with a star tip. **Makes about 4¹/₂ dozen cookies**

³/₄ cup (1¹/₂ sticks)
  unsalted butter,
  softened
¹/₂ cup sugar
2 eggs, lightly beaten
1 teaspoon vanilla
  extract
¹/₂ teaspoon
  ground cinnamon
¹/₄ teaspoon salt
2 cups all-purpose flour

²/₃ cup strawberry
  preserves, or other
  flavor if desired

1. Preheat the oven to 400°F. In a large bowl, using an electric mixer, beat the butter for 30 seconds, until creamy. Add the sugar and beat for 1–2 minutes, until light and fluffy. Gradually beat in the eggs, vanilla extract, cinnamon, and salt. Stir in the flour until a soft dough forms.

2. Spoon the dough into a large pastry bag fitted with a plain ¹/₂-inch tip. Pipe 1¹/₂-inch rounds

1 inch apart on two large, ungreased baking sheets. Press a lightly floured thumb into the center of each round, making a deep depression.

3. Bake the cookies for about 8 minutes, until golden. If the indentations begin to fill in, use the end of a wooden spoon handle to accentuate them. Remove the baking sheets to wire racks and, using a spatula, transfer the cookies to wire racks to cool.

4. While the cookies are still warm, heat the strawberry preserves in a small saucepan over low heat, until just beginning to bubble. Using a small teaspoon, spoon a little of the preserves into each indentation. Allow the cookies and preserves to set and cool completely. Store the cookies in airtight containers in single layers.

Chocolate-Dipped Lime Ribbons

To pipe cookies, the dough must be of a soft enough consistency.
In this recipe, the egg white is folded into the dough to give it just
the right texture. **Makes about 30 cookies**

Vegetable oil spray
  or vegetable oil,
  for greasing
³/₄ cup all-purpose
  flour
2 tablespoons cornstarch
¹/₈ teaspoon baking
  powder
¹/₂ cup (1 stick) unsalted
  butter, softened

¹/₃ cup confectioners'
  sugar
1 egg, separated
Grated zest of 1 large
  lime
1 tablespoon lime juice
¹/₂ teaspoon vanilla
  extract
¹/₈ teaspoon salt
Sugar, for sprinkling

4 oz. semisweet
  chocolate, melted
1 oz. pistachio
  nuts, finely
  chopped

1. Preheat the oven to 350°F. Lightly spray or grease two large baking sheets. Sift the flour, cornstarch, and baking powder in a bowl.

2. In a large bowl, using an electric mixer, beat the butter and sugar for 1–2 minutes, until light and fluffy. Beat in the egg yolk, lime zest, lime juice, and vanilla extract until well blended. Stir in the flour mixture until well blended, and set aside.

3. In a small, clean bowl, using an electric mixer with clean beaters, beat the egg white and salt until stiff peaks form. Gently fold into the dough until blended—the dough should be soft.

4. Spoon the dough into a pastry bag fitted with a medium ribbon tip. Pipe 2-inch lengths about 1 inch apart onto the baking sheets and sprinkle each cookie with a little sugar.

5. Bake for about 10 minutes, until set and the edges are golden. Remove the baking sheets to wire racks to cool for 3–5 minutes.

Using a spatula, transfer the cookies to wire racks to cool completely.

6. Dip the end of each cookie into melted chocolate and place on a waxed paper–lined baking sheet, then sprinkle with a few chopped pistachios. Allow the chocolate to set. Store the cookies in airtight containers, with waxed paper between the layers.

RIGHT: *This charming Raggedy Ann cookie jar was made by the Nelson McCoy Company.*

Mocha Meringue Rosettes

These meringue cookies are made with cocoa and instant espresso for a sophisticated mocha flavor. **Makes about 3¹/₂ dozen cookies**

2 ¹/₄ cups confectioners'
    sugar, sifted
1 teaspoon instant
    espresso powder
    (not granules)

1 ¹/₂ teaspoons
    unsweetened cocoa
    powder (preferably
    Dutch-processed)
4 egg whites
¹/₄ teaspoon cream
    of tartar
1 teaspoon vanilla
    extract

1. Line two large baking sheets with foil. In a small bowl, sift together ¹/₄ cup of the confectioners' sugar, the espresso powder, and cocoa, and set aside.

2. Preheat the oven to 200°F. In a large bowl, using an electric mixer, beat the egg whites on low speed until foamy. Add the cream of tartar and continue beating until soft peaks form. Gradually add the remaining confectioners' sugar a tablespoon at a time, beating well after each addition, until the whites are stiff and glossy; this will take 10–15 minutes. Beat in the vanilla, sprinkle over the sugar and cocoa mixture, and fold into the whites until just blended.

3. Spoon the meringue mixture into a large pastry bag fitted with a medium star tip. Pipe 2½-inch rosettes 1½ inch apart onto the prepared baking sheets. Bake for 1 hour. Turn off the oven, but do not open the door, and allow the cookies to continue to dry for another hour. Remove the baking sheets from

the oven and peel the cookies off the foil. Cool completely on wire racks. Store the rosettes in airtight containers.

TIP

○ **For even-sized rosettes, use a star cutter as a guide. Before piping, place cutter on foil and gently press to make a mark at each star tip in even rows on the foil.**

Anise Puffs

These unusual cookies are found in Italian, German, Austrian, and Jewish cookbooks. **Makes about 4 dozen cookies**

4 eggs
1 1/4 cups sugar
3–4 drops anise oil
  or lemon extract
1 tablespoon anise
  seeds, lightly crushed
Grated zest of 1 small
  lemon (optional)
2 1/2–3 cups flour,
  sifted

1. Generously grease two large baking sheets. In a large bowl, using an electric mixer, beat the eggs and sugar until very thick and "sticky" and the mixture leaves a very thick, slow ribbon trail when the beaters are lifted from the bowl, at least 15 minutes. Beat in the anise oil or lemon extract and anise seeds. On low speed, beat in the flour until a soft dough forms.

2. Spoon mixture into a large pastry bag fitted with 1/4-inch plain tip. Pipe 1–1 1/2 inch

TIP

○ There is no
raising agent in
this recipe, so
be sure to beat
the mixture until
thick and sticky,
or the cookies
won't puff.

Right: *Olive Oyl makes a great subject for a cookie jar. This jar dates from the late 1980s, although many earlier examples exist.*

mounds onto greased baking sheets. Set aside to dry overnight at room temperature.

3. Preheat the oven to 300°F. Bake for 15–20 minutes, until puffed and lightly golden, rotating the baking sheets between the top and bottom shelves, and from front to back, halfway through the cooking time. Remove baking sheets to wire racks to cool slightly. Use a metal spatula to transfer cookies to wire racks to cool completely. Store cookies in an airtight container.

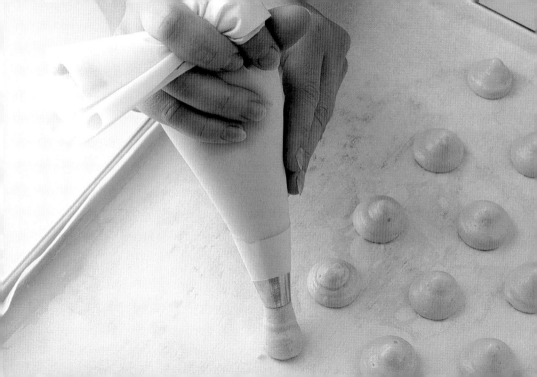

Bar
cookies

Spicy Pumpkin Bars

Although this dense, cakelike bar contains canned pumpkin, its spicy flavor and sweet-sharp topping will remind you of carrot cake. **Makes about 4 dozen bars**

2 cups all-purpose flour
2 teaspoons baking
  powder
2 teaspoons ground
  cinnamon
1 teaspoon allspice
1/2 teaspoon ground
  ginger
1/2 teaspoon ground
  cloves

1/2 teaspoon salt
1 lb. (16-oz. can)
  pumpkin
4 eggs, lightly beaten
1 3/4 cups sugar
1 cup vegetable oil
1/2 cup raisins
1/2 cup golden raisins
3/4 cup chopped
  walnuts

TOPPING
8 oz. cream cheese,
  softened
1/4 cup (1/2 stick) butter
  or margarine
1 teaspoon vanilla
  extract
1 1/2–2 cups
  confectioners' sugar
1 cup chopped walnuts

They might have been
whisked out of elf-land
—*in light are they*

Clover Leaves *Sunshine* BISCUITS

1. Preheat the oven to 350°F. Lightly grease a 15½ x 10½ x 1-inch jelly-roll pan. Line with foil (see page 256) or nonstick baking parchment and lightly grease the foil or paper.
2. In a large bowl, stir together the flour, baking powder, cinnamon, allspice, ginger, cloves, and salt. In another large bowl, using an electric mixer, beat the pumpkin on low speed to break up. Add the eggs, sugar, and oil and beat until well blended. On low speed, beat in the flour mixture, then stir in

the raisins, golden raisins, and chopped walnuts to distribute evenly. Pour into the prepared pan and smooth the top.

3. Bake for about 25 minutes, until set and golden and a toothpick inserted in the center comes out with just a few crumbs attached. Remove to a wire rack to cool completely.

4. Meanwhile, prepare the cream cheese topping. In a large bowl, using an electric mixer, beat the cream cheese, butter or margarine, and vanilla extract until well blended. On low speed, gradually beat in the sugar until smooth and spreadable (be careful not to overbeat or the topping may become grainy).

5. Spread the topping evenly over the pumpkin base and sprinkle with the chopped walnuts. Refrigerate until firm. Using the foil or paper as a guide, gently transfer to an even surface and cut into bars. Refrigerate the bars in an airtight container, with waxed paper between the layers.

Lemon Bars

These delicious lemon bars are a great favorite; they resemble the classic French tarte au citron—*lemon tart.*

Makes about 30 bars

SHORTBREAD CRUST
*Vegetable oil spray
  or vegetable oil,
  for greasing
1½ cups all-purpose
  flour*

½ cup confectioners'
  sugar
½ teaspoon salt
¾ cup (1½ sticks) cold
  unsalted butter, cut
  into small pieces
1 teaspoon grated
  lemon zest

LEMON TOPPING
4 eggs
1½ cups superfine
  sugar
Grated zest of
  1 lemon
½ cup fresh lemon juice
¾ cup heavy cream
Confectioners' sugar,
  for dusting

1. Preheat the oven to 325°F. Invert a 13 x 9-inch baking pan. Mold foil over the bottom of the pan, smoothing it evenly at the corners. Remove the foil, turn the pan right-side up, and press the foil into it, smoothing into the sides and corners. Spray or grease.

2. Sift the flour, sugar, and salt in a large bowl. Sprinkle with the butter and lemon

LEFT: *This unusual and rather glamorous train cookie jar was made by Sierra Vista.*

zest. Using a pastry blender or fingertips, cut in the butter until coarse crumbs form and the dough begins to stick together.

3. Turn into the pan and pat firmly over the bottom to form an even layer, smoothing the surface. Bake for about 20 minutes, until just golden. Remove the pan to a wire rack to cool slightly.

4. In a medium bowl, beat the eggs and sugar for 3–5 minutes, until fluffy. Beat in the lemon zest and juice.

5. In another bowl, using clean beaters, beat the cream until soft peaks form. Fold into the egg mixture in two batches and pour over the base. Return the pan to the oven and bake for about 40 minutes, until the topping is set. Remove the pan to a wire rack to cool.

6. Using the foil as a guide, remove from the pan and set on a board. Peel off the foil and cut into bars. Dust the tops of the bars lightly with confectioners' sugar.

Fruit Bars

These chewy bars are packed with lots of fruits and spice for extra flavor—great for picnics and the kids' lunch boxes. **Makes about 1 dozen bars**

*Vegetable oil spray
or vegetable oil,
for greasing*
½ cup (1 stick) butter
*⅓ cup packed light
brown sugar*
*2 tablespoons dark
corn syrup*
2 tablespoons molasses
*2 cups quick-cooking
oats*

*1 teaspoon ground
cinnamon*
*2 tablespoons dried
apricots, finely chopped*
*2 tablespoons dried
pitted dates, finely
chopped*

1. Preheat the oven to 350°F. Invert an 8-inch square baking pan. Mold a sheet of foil over the bottom of the pan. Remove the foil, turn the pan right-side up, and press the foil into the pan, smoothing it evenly into the corners. Spray or grease the foil.

2. In a medium saucepan over medium-low heat, melt the butter, sugar, corn syrup, and molasses, stirring frequently. Remove from the heat and add the oats, ground cinnamon, apricots, and dates, and stir until well blended.

3. Spread the mixture in the pan and smooth the top. Bake for 30–35 minutes, until lightly browned. Allow to cool slightly and mark into bars. Using the foil, remove from the pan and cut into bars. Arrange on a wire rack to cool. Store in an airtight container.

RIGHT: *One of many Dutch Girl cookie jars, this popular design is coveted by collectors.*

Fudgy Peanut Butter Brownies

These brownies will satisfy the sweetest sweet tooth.

Makes 12–16 brownies

6 oz. unsweetened
  chocolate
1 cup (2 sticks) butter
2 cups sugar
4 eggs
2 teaspoons vanilla
  extract
½ cup all-purpose flour
¼ teaspoon salt
1 cup semisweet
  chocolate chips

PEANUT BUTTER
LAYER

1½ cups peanut butter,
  smooth or chunky
½ cup (1 stick) butter,
  softened
1 cup (6 oz.) peanut
  butter chips or
  white chocolate
  chips

½ cup confectioners'
  sugar, plus extra
  for dusting

RIGHT: *This
spaceship cookie
jar holds out-of-
the-world cookies.*

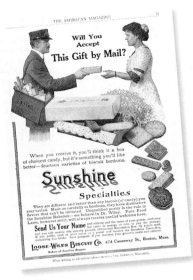

1. Invert an 8-inch square baking pan and mold a piece of foil over the bottom of the pan, smoothing it evenly around the corners. Remove the foil and turn the pan right-side up. Press the foil into the pan, smoothing it into the sides and corners.

2. In a medium saucepan over medium-low heat, melt the chocolate and butter, stirring frequently until smooth. Remove from the heat and stir in the sugar until it begins to dissolve. Beat in the eggs, then stir in the vanilla extract, flour, salt, and chocolate chips until just blended. Spoon half the brownie batter into the pan and smooth evenly. Freeze for 15–20 minutes, until the surface is firm. Preheat the oven to 350°F.

3. Prepare the peanut butter layer. In a medium bowl, using an electric mixer, beat the peanut butter and butter for about 2 minutes, until well blended. Gradually beat in the chips and confectioners' sugar. Spoon the mixture evenly over the brownie layer. Spoon the remaining brownie mixture over the peanut butter layer and smooth evenly.

4. Bake for 35–40 minutes, until the surface is puffed and just set. Remove to a wire rack to cool completely. Using the foil, lift the brownies out of the pan and set on a work surface. Dust with confectioners' sugar before cutting into squares.

RIGHT: *Chewy Caramel Nut Squares and Butterscotch Bars*

Butterscotch Bars with Meringue Topping

A walnut-enriched, crackly meringue topping covers a butterscotch cookie layer—sweet but irresistible! **Makes about 1 dozen bars**

COOKIE LAYER

Vegetable oil spray
  or vegetable oil,
  for greasing

¼ cup (½ stick)
  unsalted butter

1 cup packed dark
  brown sugar

½ cup all-purpose flour

1 teaspoon ground
  cinnamon

½ teaspoon salt

1 egg

1 teaspoon vanilla
  extract

MERINGUE TOPPING

1 egg white

⅛ teaspoon cream of
  tartar

1 tablespoon corn
  syrup

½ cup superfine sugar

1 cup chopped
  walnuts

1. Preheat the oven to 350°F. Invert an 8-inch square baking pan. Mold a sheet of foil over the bottom of the pan, smoothing it evenly around the corners. Remove the foil and turn the pan right-side up. Press the foil into the pan, smoothing it into the sides and corners. Spray or grease the foil.

2. In a medium saucepan over medium heat, simmer the butter and brown sugar for about 3–5 minutes, until the sugar dissolves. Remove from the heat and cool.

Sift the flour, cinnamon, and salt in a medium bowl.

3. Beat the egg and vanilla extract into the cooled butter mixture until well blended. Stir in the flour mixture until just blended. Spread over the bottom of the pan, smoothing the surface evenly.

4. In a medium bowl, beat the egg white until foamy. Add the cream of tartar and continue beating until soft peaks form. Gradually beat in the corn syrup, then the sugar, and continue beating until the whites are stiff and glossy. Fold in half the nuts and spread the topping over the butterscotch layer. Sprinkle with the remaining nuts.

5. Bake for about 30 minutes, until the topping is puffed (the meringue may crack) and golden. Remove to a wire rack and cool completely. Using the foil as a guide, remove to a board and peel off the foil. Cut into 1½-inch fingers. Store in airtight containers in single layers.

Chewy Caramel Nut Squares

This chewy bar cookie is a nut lover's dream. A rich, honey-flavored caramel topping, filled with a combination of nuts, covers a rich pastry. **Makes about 3 dozen squares**

PASTRY CRUST
Vegetable oil spray
  or vegetable oil,
  for greasing

3 cups all-purpose flour
1/2 cup cornstarch
1/2 teaspoon salt
1 1/2 cups (3 sticks)
  unsalted butter,
  softened

2/3 cup sugar
Grated zest of 1 lemon

CARAMEL NUT TOPPING
10 tablespoons
  (1 1/4 sticks) unsalted
  butter
1/2 cup packed dark
  brown sugar
1/2 cup honey

1 1/2 tablespoons
  whipping cream
1 cup salted cashews,
  lightly toasted and
  coarsely chopped
1 cup whole blanched
  almonds, toasted
  and coarsely chopped
1 cup pine nuts,
  toasted

1. Invert a 13 x 9-inch baking pan. Mold foil over the bottom, smoothing it evenly around the corners. Remove the foil and turn the pan right-side up. Press the foil into the pan, smoothing it into the sides and corners. Spray or grease the foil.

2. Preheat the oven to 350°F. Sift the flour, cornstarch, and salt into a medium bowl. In a large bowl, using an electric mixer, beat the butter, sugar, and lemon zest for 1–2 minutes, until light and fluffy. On low speed, beat in the flour mixture, until well blended and a soft dough forms.

3. Press the dough evenly onto the bottom and 1 inch up the sides of the pan, pressing into the corners. Prick the bottom with

a fork and bake for about 30 minutes, until the pastry is very lightly browned, turning the pan halfway through cooking and pricking with a fork if the pastry puffs up. Remove the pan to a wire rack.

4. In a medium saucepan over medium heat, bring to a boil the butter, sugar, honey, and cream, stirring until the sugar dissolves. Boil, without stirring, for about 1 minute, until the mixture thickens slightly.

Remove from the heat and stir in the cashews, almonds, and pine nuts until well mixed.

5. Pour the nut mixture over the crust, spreading evenly. Bake for about 20 minutes, until sticky and bubbling. Remove to a wire rack to cool completely. Using the foil as a guide, remove to a board. Carefully peel off the foil and cut into 1½-inch squares. Store in airtight containers in single layers.

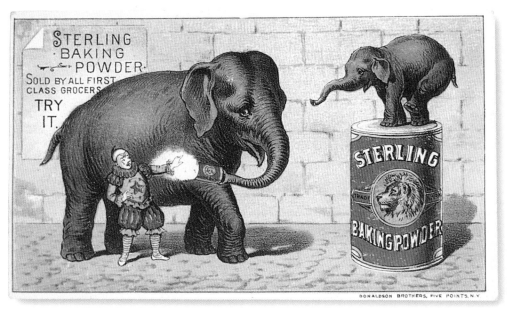

Scottish Shortbread

This famous Scottish cookie is simple but so good. Because there are few ingredients, they must be first-class, so buy the best butter. **Makes 16 large wedges or 32 thin wedges**

Vegetable oil spray or
  butter, for greasing
¼ cup confectioners'
  sugar
¼ cup superfine sugar
¼ teaspoon salt
10 tablespoons
  (1 ¼ sticks) unsalted
  butter, softened
1 ½ cups all-purpose
  flour

1. Preheat the oven to 275°F. Lightly spray or brush with softened butter two 8-inch tart or cake pans with removable bottoms. Sift the confectioners' sugar into a large bowl. Add the superfine sugar and salt, and mix well. Add the butter and, using an electric mixer, beat the butter and sugars for 1–2 minutes, until light and fluffy. Stir in the flour in 2–3 batches until well blended. On a lightly floured surface, knead the

dough very lightly to ensure an even blending.

2. Divide the dough evenly between the pans and pat onto the bottoms in even layers. Using a kitchen fork, press ¾-inch radiating lines around the edge of the dough. Prick the surface lightly with a fork (this helps keep an even surface as well as creating

the traditional pattern). If you like, score each shortbread dough round into eight or sixteen wedges for easier cutting later.

3. Bake for about 40 minutes, until pale golden (do not brown—shortbread should be very pale), rotating the pans halfway through cooking. Reduce the oven temperature if the

shortbread begins to color too quickly.
Remove the pans to a wire rack to cool
for 10 minutes.

4. Carefully remove the side of each pan
and place the pan bottoms onto a heatproof
surface. Cut each circle into eight wide or
sixteen thin wedges, using the scored
marks, if used. This must be done while
the shortbread is warm and soft, or it will
break. Return the wedges on their bases
to wire racks to cool completely.

LEFT: *The
Metlox Mama
Kangaroo is a
relatively rare
cookie jar.*

Rocky Road Bars

This is a great bar cookie, like a rich, crunchy brownie with a chocolate, marshmallow, and nut topping. It's gooey and difficult to cut, but no one cares! **Makes about 2 dozen bars**

Vegetable oil spray
   or vegetable oil,
   for greasing
1³/₄ cups all-purpose
   flour
¹/₄ cup unsweetened
   cocoa powder
   (preferably
   Dutch-processed)

1 teaspoon baking
   soda
¹/₂ teaspoon salt
1 cup (2 sticks)
   unsalted butter,
   softened
1 cup packed light
   brown sugar
2 eggs, lightly beaten

1 teaspoon vanilla
   extract
³/₄ cup sweetened
   flaked coconut
3 cups semisweet
   chocolate chips
1 cup whole blanched
   almonds, chopped
1 cup mini marshmallows

1. Preheat the oven to 350°F. Invert a 13 x 9-inch baking pan. Mold a sheet of foil over the bottom of the pan, smoothing it evenly around the corners. Remove the foil and turn the pan right-side up. Press the foil into the pan, smoothing it into the sides and corners. Spray or grease the foil.

2. In a medium bowl, sift the flour, cocoa powder, baking soda, and salt. In a large bowl, using an electric mixer, beat the butter and sugar for about 1 minute, until light and fluffy. Beat in the eggs and vanilla extract. On low speed, beat in the flour-cocoa mixture until well blended, then stir in the coconut, 2 cups of the chocolate chips, and ¾ cup of the chopped almonds.

3. Turn the mixture into the prepared pan and spread evenly. Bake for about 15 minutes, until set but still moist in the center. Remove the pan from the oven and sprinkle the top evenly with the remaining chocolate chips, the chopped almonds, and the marshmallows.

Return the pan to the oven and bake for about 4 minutes, until the chocolate and marshmallows begin to soften and blend into each other. Remove to a wire rack to cool for 10 minutes.

4. Using the foil as a guide, remove to a board. Peel off the foil and, while still warm, cut into bars. Cool on a wire rack, although these bars are fantastic while still slightly warm. Store in an airtight container, with waxed paper between the layers.

Toffee Bars

Kids love these rich, sticky bars, so you may have to keep that cookie jar hidden.

Makes about 1 dozen bars

Vegetable oil spray
  or vegetable oil,
  for greasing

COOKIE BASE
1/2 cup (1 stick) butter
1/4 cup sugar
1 1/2 cups all-purpose
  flour, sifted

TOFFEE CARAMEL
1/2 cup (1 stick) butter
1/4 cup sugar
2 1/2 tablespoons corn
  syrup
2/3 cup condensed milk

CHOCOLATE TOPPING
4 oz. semisweet
  chocolate
1 tablespoon butter

1. Preheat the oven to 350°F. Invert an 8-inch square baking pan. Mold a sheet of foil over the bottom of the pan. Remove the foil, turn the pan right-side up, and press the foil into the pan, smoothing it evenly into the corners. Spray or grease the foil.

2. In a medium bowl, using an electric mixer, beat the butter and sugar until light and fluffy. Add the flour and stir until a smooth dough forms. Spread the dough evenly into the pan and prick all over with a fork. Bake for 20–25 minutes, until the edges are lightly browned. Remove to a wire rack to cool.

3. In a medium saucepan over low heat, melt the ingredients for the toffee caramel, stirring constantly until smooth. Bring slowly to a boil and cook for 5 more minutes, stirring constantly.

Set aside to cool slightly, then spread over the cookie base and leave to set.

4. In a small saucepan over low heat, melt the chocolate and butter until smooth. Carefully spread the toffee on top and allow to set before cutting into bars. Store the bars in airtight containers, with waxed paper between the layers.

Cranberry Squares

This is a good cupboard recipe for when you have that unexpected urge to bake something sweet but simple. **Makes about 1 dozen squares**

Vegetable oil spray
  or vegetable oil,
  for greasing
¹/₂ cup (1 stick) butter
¹/₂ cup packed dark
  brown sugar
1 cup all-purpose flour,
  sifted
¹/₄ teaspoon salt

1 cup old-fashioned
  rolled oats
¹/₂ cup cranberry sauce
¹/₂ cup walnuts, chopped

RIGHT: *This Winnie
the Pooh Honey Pot jar
by California Originals
is an old favorite.*

1. Preheat the oven to 350°F. Invert an 8-inch square baking pan. Mold a sheet of foil over the bottom of the pan. Remove the foil, turn the pan right-side up, and press the foil into the pan, smoothing it evenly into the corners. Spray or grease the foil.

2. In a medium bowl, using an electric mixer, beat the butter and sugar until light and fluffy. Stir in the flour, salt, and oats until well blended. Spread two thirds of the mixture evenly over the bottom of the pan.

3. In a small bowl, combine the cranberry sauce and nuts, and spread evenly over the oat mixture. Spoon the remaining oat mixture evenly over the top and gently press into the cranberry filling.

4. Bake for about 20 minutes. Remove to a wire rack to cool for 10 minutes, then mark into squares or bars. Leave to cool completely in the pan. Using the foil as a guide, remove from the pan. Cut into squares or bars as marked. Store in an airtight container.

A Touch of Sweetness with the Flavor of Lemon

NATIONAL BISCUIT COMPANY

Lemon Snaps 5¢

IN·ER SEAL

5¢
NATIONAL
BISCUIT COMPANY

RIGHT:

Chocolate-Pecan
Brownies and
Chocolate
Raspberry
Macaroon Bars

Chocolate-Pecan Brownies

Brownies must be dense and fudgy; adding more chocolate, pecans, and a dark, buttery, chocolate glaze makes them even more special. **Makes 2 dozen squares**

Vegetable oil spray
or vegetable oil,
for greasing
4 oz. unsweetened
chocolate, chopped
¾ cup (1½ sticks)
butter, cut into pieces
1¾ cups sugar
3 eggs
1 teaspoon vanilla
extract

1½ cups pecans
1 cup semisweet
chocolate chips
1 cup all-purpose flour

CHOCOLATE GLAZE
6 oz. bittersweet
chocolate, chopped
½ cup heavy cream
2 tablespoons unsalted
butter, cut into pieces

1 teaspoon vanilla
extract
24 perfect pecan halves,
to decorate (optional)

1. Preheat the oven to 350°F. Invert a 13 x 9-inch baking pan. Mold a sheet of foil over the bottom of the pan. Remove the foil and turn the pan right-side up. Press the foil into the pan, smoothing it into the sides and corners. Lightly spray or grease.

2. Melt the chocolate and butter in a medium saucepan over low heat, until melted and smooth, stirring frequently. Remove from the heat and stir in the sugar until blended. Beat in the eggs, one at a time, beating well after each addition. Stir in the vanilla extract, nuts, and chocolate chips. Stir in the flour until just blended—the batter will be stiff. Spread the batter in the pan, smoothing the top evenly.

3. Bake for about 25 minutes, until a cake tester or toothpick inserted in the center comes out with sticky crumbs attached. Be very careful not to overbake the brownies. Remove from the pan to a wire rack to cool completely.

4. Melt the chocolate and cream in a medium saucepan over low heat, until melted and smooth, stirring frequently. Remove from the heat to cool slightly. Whisk in the butter and vanilla extract. Cool the remaining glaze until thickened and spreadable.

5. Using the foil as a guide, remove the brownies from the pan and invert onto a board. Using a thin-bladed metal spatula, spread the brownies with the glaze. Refrigerate for at least 1 hour, until set.

Using a sharp knife, cut the brownies into twenty-four squares. Press a pecan half into the center of each brownie square, if using. Store in airtight containers in single layers.

TIP
○ **For easy unglazed brownies, refrigerate for 1 hour before cutting into squares. Dust the squares with confectioners' sugar.**

Chocolate Raspberry Macaroon Bars

*A dark chocolate crust filled with raspberry preserves and an almond topping
bakes to a chewy texture.* **Makes about 2 dozen bars**

COOKIE CRUST
Vegetable oil spray
  or vegetable oil,
  for greasing
1/2 cup (1 stick) unsalted
  butter, softened
1/2 cup confectioners'
  sugar, sifted
1/4 cup unsweetened cocoa
  powder, sifted
1/4 teaspoon salt

1 teaspoon vanilla or
  almond extract
1 cup all-purpose flour

FILLING
1/2 cup seedless raspberry
  preserves
1 tablespoon raspberry
  flavor liqueur (optional)
1 cup mini semisweet or
  milk chocolate chips

1 1/2 cups finely ground
  blanched almonds
4 egg whites
1/4 teaspoon salt
1 cup superfine sugar
1/2 teaspoon almond
  extract
1/4 cup slivered almonds
Confectioners' sugar, for
  dusting (optional)

1. Preheat the oven to 325°F. Invert a 13 x 9-inch baking pan. Mold foil over the bottom of the pan, smoothing it evenly around the corners. Remove the foil and turn the pan right-side up. Press the foil into the pan, smoothing it into the sides and corners. Spray or grease the foil.

RIGHT: *This jolly-looking creature is the Brush Happy Bunny cookie jar.*

2. In a medium bowl, using an electric mixer, beat the butter, sugar, cocoa powder, and salt for 1–2 minutes, until creamy. Beat in the vanilla or almond extract. On low speed, beat in the flour until a crumbly dough forms.
3. Turn the dough into the pan and pat firmly over the bottom to create an even layer. Prick the dough with a fork. Bake for about 20 minutes, until set. Remove the dough from the oven to a wire rack and increase the oven temperature to 375°F.

4. Combine the raspberry preserves and liqueur in a small bowl. Spread evenly over the crust, then sprinkle with the chocolate chips.

5. Put the ground almonds, egg whites, salt, superfine sugar, and almond extract in a food processor. Using a metal blade, process the ingredients. Gently pour over the raspberry–chocolate chip layer, spreading evenly to the sides of the pan. Sprinkle with the slivered almonds.

6. Bake for about 25 minutes, until the top is lightly browned and puffed. Remove to a wire rack and cool for about half an hour, until firm enough to handle. Using the foil as a guide, remove from the pan and cool on a wire rack. When cool, peel off the foil and place on a board. Cut into bars and dust with confectioners' sugar, if you like. Store in airtight containers in single layers.

Lemon Cheesecake Squares

This classic New York–style cheesecake topping on a pecan crust makes delicious yet delicate cookies. They remain slightly soft, so be careful cutting them. **Makes about 16 squares**

PECAN CRUST

1 cup all-purpose flour

½ cup pecans, finely
  chopped

⅓ cup packed light
  brown sugar

6 tablespoons (¾ stick)
  unsalted butter,
  softened

CHEESECAKE TOPPING

8 oz. cream cheese,
  softened

¼ cup sugar

1 tablespoon sour cream

Grated zest of 1 lemon

1 tablespoon lemon juice

1 teaspoon vanilla extract

1 egg

½ cup pecans, chopped

RIGHT: *This wacky jar is called "Man with a Chicken on his Head."*

1. Preheat the oven to 350°F. Invert a 9-inch square baking pan. Mold a sheet of foil over the bottom of the pan, smoothing evenly around the corners. Remove the foil and turn the pan right-side up. Press the foil into the pan, smoothing it into the sides and corners.
2. In a medium bowl, stir together the flour, chopped pecans, and sugar. Add the butter

LEFT: *Noah's Ark is the inspiration behind the design of this lovely jar.*

and, with a pastry blender or fingertips, cut in until crumbs form and stick together when pressed between two fingers. Press evenly into the bottom of the foil-lined pan. Bake for 12–15 minutes, until golden. Remove to a wire rack.

3. In a medium bowl, using an electric mixer, beat the softened cream cheese and sugar for about 1 minute, until light and fluffy. Beat in the sour cream, lemon zest and juice, vanilla extract, and egg until well blended. Pour the mixture over the baked crust and sprinkle with the chopped pecans.

4. Bake for 25 minutes, until puffed and golden. Remove to a wire rack to cool completely, then refrigerate for 2–3 hours until well chilled. Using the foil as a guide, remove to a board. Peel off the foil and, with a sharp knife, cut into squares. Store refrigerated in airtight containers in single layers.

Date-Filled Oat Crumb Squares

*This delicious bar cookie is a mixture of an oaty base and crumbly topping
with a rich date puree filling.* **Makes about 2 dozen squares**

FILLING

1 lb. pitted dates

1 cup packed light brown
 sugar

1 cup water

1 teaspoon vanilla
 extract

1/2 teaspoon ground
 cinnamon

CRUST

Vegetable oil spray
 or vegetable oil,
 for greasing

1 1/2 cups old-fashioned
 rolled oats

1 1/2 cups all-purpose
 flour

1 cup packed light brown
 sugar

1 teaspoon ground
 cinnamon

1/2 teaspoon baking soda

1/2 cup chopped walnuts
 or pecans

1 cup (2 sticks) cold
 unsalted butter, cut
 into small pieces

1. Simmer the dates, sugar, and water in a medium saucepan over medium heat until the sugar dissolves and all the liquid is evaporated. Remove from the heat and stir in the vanilla extract and cinnamon. Pour into a food processor and, using a metal blade, process the mixture until just smooth. Pour into a bowl to cool.

2. Invert a 13 x 9-inch baking pan. Mold foil over the bottom, smoothing it evenly around the corners. Remove the foil and turn the pan right-side up. Press the foil into the pan, smoothing into the sides and corners. Spray or grease the foil.

3. Preheat the oven to 350°F. In a large bowl, combine the oats, flour, brown sugar, cinnamon, baking soda, and walnuts or pecans. Sprinkle over the cut-up butter and, using a pastry blender or your fingertips, cut in the butter until coarse crumbs form.

4. Turn half the mixture into the pan and pat firmly into the bottom and sides to form a lower crust, smoothing the surface. Spread the filling evenly over the crust, then sprinkle over the remaining crumb mixture, distributing it evenly over the filling.

5. Bake for about 35 minutes, until the topping is browned and the filling is sizzling. Remove the pan to a wire rack to cool for about 1 hour. Using the foil as a guide, remove from the pan and set on a board. Peel off the foil and cut into squares. Store in airtight containers.

Chocolate Chip–Pecan Shortbread Triangles

This is a rich shortbread laced with chocolate chips and finely ground pecans. It is one of the most popular cookies and never lasts long. **Makes about 32 triangles**

1 cup pecans, toasted
  and cooled
1 3/4 cups all-purpose
  flour
1/4 cup cornstarch

1/2 cup confectioners'
  sugar
1/4 teaspoon salt
1 cup (2 sticks) unsalted
  butter, softened
1 cup mini semisweet
  chocolate chips
1 1/2 oz . semisweet
  chocolate, melted

1. Preheat the oven to 325°F. Lightly grease two 8-inch tart pans with removable bottoms. In a food processor fitted with a metal blade, process the toasted pecans until very fine crumbs form; do not overprocess or the nuts may become pasty and oily. Pour into a large bowl.

2. Sift the flour, cornstarch, confectioners' sugar, and salt into the ground nuts and mix well. Add the butter and, using a pastry cutter or your fingertips, cut in until the dough holds together. Stir in the chocolate chips.

3. Divide the dough evenly between the tart pans and pat onto the bottom in an even layer, carefully smoothing the surface. Bake for about 20 minutes, until the edges are golden and the surface appears slightly puffed. Remove the pans to wire racks to cool for about 5 minutes.

4. Carefully remove the side of each pan and place the pan bottom and shortbread on a heatproof surface. Cut each circle into sixteen thin triangles; this must be done while the shortbread is warm and soft or it will break. Return the triangles, on their bases, to wire racks to cool completely.

5. Using a metal palette knife, transfer the shortbread triangles to a wire rack, arranging them top-to-toe to fit close together. Spoon melted chocolate into a paper cone (see page 81) and drizzle over the triangles. Store in airtight containers, with waxed paper between the layers.

Chocolate-Orange Dream Bars

Chocolate and orange is a classic combination. Here, a rich orange curd topping contrasts perfectly with a crisp chocolate crust. **Makes about 18 bars**

CHOCOLATE CRUST

1 cup all-purpose flour

1/4 cup unsweetened
  cocoa powder

1/4 teaspoon salt

10 tablespoons
  (1 1/4 sticks) unsalted
  butter, softened

1/3 cup superfine sugar

1/3 cup confectioners'
  sugar

ORANGE FILLING

Grated zest of 1 orange

1/2 cup fresh orange juice

1/4 cup water

4 teaspoons cornstarch

1 teaspoon lemon juice

1 tablespoon butter

1/2 cup orange
  marmalade

CHOCOLATE GLAZE

3 tablespoons heavy
  cream

1/2 teaspoon corn
  syrup

3 oz. bittersweet or
  semisweet chocolate,
  chopped

1. Preheat the oven to 325°F. Invert an 8-inch square baking pan. Mold a sheet of foil over the bottom, smoothing it evenly around the corners. Remove the foil and turn pan right-side up. Press the foil into the pan, smoothing it into the sides and corners.

2. In a medium bowl, sift the flour, cocoa powder, and salt. In a large bowl, using an electric mixer, beat the butter and sugars for about 1 minute, until light and fluffy. On low speed, in two or three batches, beat in the flour mixture until well blended and a soft dough forms.

3. Pat the dough onto the bottom of the prepared pan in an even layer, smoothing the surface. Prick the dough all over with a fork. Bake for about 30 minutes, until the crust is set and lightly colored. Remove to a wire rack to cool slightly.

4. Meanwhile, in a medium saucepan, whisk together the orange zest and juice, water, cornstarch, and lemon juice. Over medium heat, bring to a boil, whisking constantly for about 1 minute, until the mixture thickens. Remove from the heat and whisk in the butter and marmalade until melted and smooth. Pour the filling over the warm crust, return it to the oven, and bake for 5 more minutes. Remove to a wire rack to cool completely, then refrigerate for about 1 hour to set the topping.

5. In a small saucepan, bring the cream and corn syrup to a boil. Remove from the heat

and, all at once, stir in the chocolate until melted and smooth. Cool the chocolate slightly until thickened, stirring occasionally.

6. Using the foil as a guide, remove from the pan and set on a board. Peel off the foil and cut into bars or squares. Spoon the cooled thickened chocolate into a paper cone (page 81) and drizzle the bars or squares with the chocolate. Refrigerate for about 30 minutes, until the chocolate sets. Store refrigerated in airtight containers in single layers.

Pear and Apricot Bars

These bars are sophisticated enough to be served with whipped cream as a dessert. **Makes about 1 dozen bars**

*Vegetable oil spray
  or vegetable oil,
  for greasing
3 pears
1½ cups dried apricots,
  finely chopped
2 tablespoons clear
  honey
1 tablespoon applesauce
2 tablespoons light
  vegetable oil*

*2 medium eggs, beaten
1½ cups whole-wheat
  flour
1½ teaspoons baking
  powder
Slivered almonds, to
  decorate*

Right: *Cookie in hand,
this Mona Lisa jar
tempts you to indulge.*

1. Preheat the oven to 375°F. Invert an 8-inch square baking pan. Mold a sheet of foil over the bottom of the pan, smoothing it evenly around the corners. Remove the foil, turn the pan right-side up, and press the foil into the pan, smoothing it into the sides and corners. Spray or grease the foil.

2. Peel and core the pears, then chop them into small pieces. Put the chopped pears in a large bowl with the finely chopped apricots, honey, and applesauce. Add the oil and beaten egg to the fruit mixture and stir until well blended.

3. Sift the flour and baking powder in a bowl and gently fold into the pear and apricot mixture. Pour the mixture into the pan, spread evenly, and sprinkle with the almonds. Bake for 25–30 minutes, until puffed and golden. Remove to a wire rack to cool completely. Using the foil as a guide, remove from the pan to a board and cut into bars. Store in an airtight container.

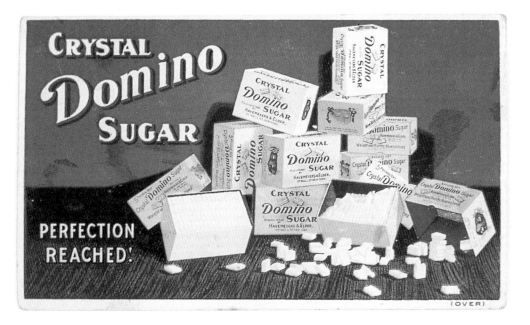

Super Fudge Brownies

These brownies are very fudgy and easy to make. They can be decorated with white chocolate, but beware—they are already very rich. **Makes about 20 brownies**

Vegetable oil spray
  or vegetable oil,
  for greasing
½ cup (1 stick) butter
4 oz. unsweetened
  chocolate, chopped
2 cups sugar
4 large eggs, beaten
1 cup less 1 tablespoon
  all-purpose flour

1 teaspoon baking
  powder
¼ teaspoon salt
1 teaspoon vanilla
  extract
¾ cup chopped pecans
  or walnuts

1. Preheat the oven to 350°F. Invert a 13 x 9-inch baking pan. Mold foil over the bottom, smoothing it evenly around the corners. Remove the foil and turn the pan right-side up. Press the foil into the pan, smoothing it into the sides and corners. Spray or grease the foil.

2. In a medium saucepan over low heat, melt the butter and chocolate until smooth. Remove from the heat and stir in the sugar. Beat in the eggs one at a time, beating well after each addition. Sift the flour, baking powder, and salt in a bowl. Stir into the chocolate mixture until well blended, then stir in the vanilla extract and nuts.

3. Pour the mixture into the pan, spreading evenly. Bake for 25–30 minutes, until moist and fudgy. A cake tester or toothpick inserted in the center should come out with sticky crumbs attached. Remove to a wire rack to cool completely. Using the foil as a guide, remove from the pan. Cut into squares.

Special *cookies*

Raspberry Rugelach

This traditional Jewish-American cookie is made with a tender cream cheese pastry. **Makes about 5½ dozen cookies**

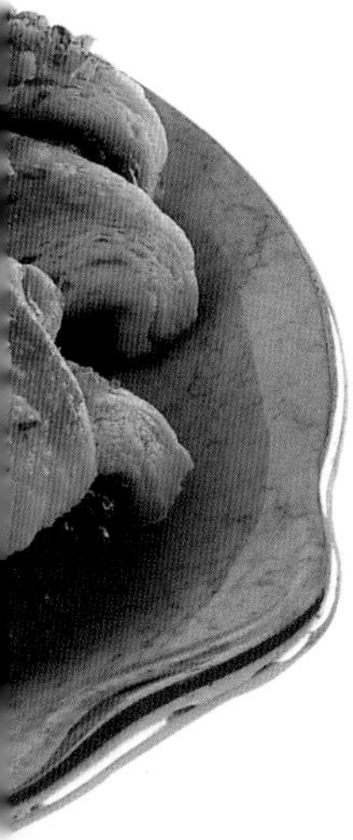

2 cups all-purpose flour

½ teaspoon salt

½ cup (1 stick) unsalted butter, softened

4 oz. cream cheese, softened

¼ cup sour cream

3 tablespoons superfine sugar

1 egg, separated

Vegetable oil spray or vegetable oil, for greasing

1 cup seedless raspberry preserves

½ cup mini white chocolate chips or 3 oz. chopped semisweet chocolate

¼ cup finely chopped, unblanched almonds

¼ cup sugar

1. Sift the flour and salt into a bowl. In another bowl, using an electric mixer, beat the butter, cream cheese, sour cream, sugar, and the egg yolk until creamy and smooth. Stir in the flour until a soft dough forms and holds together. Knead lightly to blend. Shape the dough into a ball and flatten to a circle. Wrap tightly in plastic wrap and refrigerate for 1–2 hours, until firm enough to handle.

2. Preheat the oven to 350°F. Lightly spray or grease two large baking sheets. On a lightly floured surface, using a floured rolling pin, roll one fourth of the dough ⅛ inch thick. Refrigerate the remaining dough. Using a 10-inch plate as a guide, cut the dough into a 10-inch circle. Spread the circle with about 3 tablespoons of raspberry preserves to within ½ inch of the edge of the dough. Sprinkle with a few chocolate chips.

3. Cut the circle into twelve equal wedges. Starting at the curved edge, roll up each wedge, jelly-roll fashion, to resemble a croissant.

Place the cookies, point side down, 1½ inches apart on one of the baking sheets. In a small bowl, beat the egg white with 1 tablespoon of water and brush each cookie with a little of the glaze. Sprinkle each cookie with chopped almonds and a little sugar.

4. Bake for 20–25 minutes, until puffed and golden brown, rotating the cookie sheet from front to back halfway through the cooking time. Remove the baking sheet to a wire rack and, using a thin-bladed metal spatula, place the cookies on a wire rack to cool. Repeat with the remaining cookie dough and trimmings. Store in airtight containers, with waxed paper between each layer.

Chocolate Cream Brandy Snaps

These sophisticated cookies can be stored and filled with cream when required.

Makes about 2¹/₂ dozen cookies

COOKIES

Butter, for greasing

¹/₂ cup (1 stick) unsalted
  butter, cut into pieces

2 tablespoons corn syrup

¹/₄ cup sugar

¹/₄ cup packed light
  brown sugar

1 teaspoon ground ginger

2 tablespoons brandy

¹/₂ cup all-purpose flour

WHIPPED CREAMS

1¹/₄ cups whipping
  cream

¹/₂ teaspoon vanilla
  extract

2 oz. bittersweet or
  semisweet chocolate,
  melted

2 oz. white chocolate,
  melted

1. Preheat the oven to 350°F. Generously grease two large baking sheets (or more if you have them), or use nonstick baking sheets. Lightly oil two wooden spoon handles. In a heavy-based saucepan over medium heat, bring the butter, corn syrup, sugars, and ginger to a boil, stirring constantly until the sugars dissolve. Remove from the heat and stir in the brandy and flour until well blended and smooth. Place the pan in a shallow bowl of hot water.

2. Begin by working in batches of no more than four cookies on each sheet. Drop tablespoonfuls of batter about 6 inches apart onto the buttered or nonstick baking sheets. Using the back of a moistened spoon, spread each mound into about 3-inch rounds (the cookies will spread more during baking). Bake for 7–10 minutes, until golden and bubbling, turning the baking sheet if the cookies begin to brown unevenly.

3. Remove the baking sheet to a wire rack and cool for about 1 minute. Working quickly, use a thin-bladed metal spatula to loosen the edge of a hot cookie and lift it from the sheet. Roll the cookie around the oiled handle of one of the wooden spoons, pressing down on

the seam for a few seconds. Repeat with another cookie; you can fit two cookies on each spoon, or do them one at a time.

4. Slide the cookies off the spoon handles and place on a wire rack to cool completely. Repeat with the remaining cookies. If they become too brittle to roll, return the baking sheet to the oven for 30 seconds. The cookies should be flexible but firm enough to lift off without wrinkling and tearing. Repeat the process with the remaining batter.

5. Up to 2 hours before serving, in a large bowl, using an electric mixer, beat the cream and vanilla extract until stiff peaks form. Quickly fold half the cream into the melted bittersweet or semisweet chocolate until completely blended. Fold the remaining cream into the melted white chocolate. Spoon the dark chocolate cream into a medium pastry bag fitted with a medium star tip. Pipe cream into both ends of half the cookies and place on a baking sheet. Spoon

the white chocolate cream into another
pastry bag fitted with a medium star tip and
pipe into both ends of the remaining cookies.
Refrigerate until ready to serve. Do not fill
the brandy snaps too early or the moisture
will soften them. Arrange on a plate to serve.
Store unfilled cookies in airtight containers,
with waxed paper between the layers.

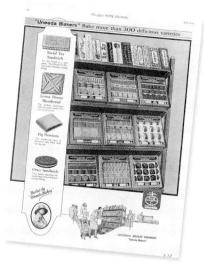

Lemon Cookie Tarts

These melt-in-the-mouth cookies are made from a sweet, lemony cookie dough and tart lemon curd. Store-bought raspberry or apricot preserves could be used instead of the lemon curd. **Makes about 36 tarts**

COOKIE DOUGH
1/2 cup (1 stick) unsalted
  butter, softened
1/2 cup superfine sugar
1 egg yolk
Grated zest of 1 lemon
1/2 teaspoon lemon
  extract
1 3/4 cups all-purpose
  flour

LEMON CURD
3/4 cup sugar
1/3 cup water
1/4 cup all-purpose flour
Grated zest and juice
  of 1 lemon
1/8 teaspoon salt
2 eggs, lightly beaten
Lemon zest, to decorate
  (optional)

RIGHT: *This
nostalgic cookie
jar is called
"Grandma's
Christmas
Cookies."*

Making your Baking Better with Karo

1. In a large bowl, beat the butter for about 1 minute, until creamy. Add the sugar and beat for 1–2 minutes, until light and fluffy. Beat in the egg yolk, lemon zest, and extract. On low speed, beat in the flour until a soft dough forms, scraping down the sides of the bowl occasionally. Refrigerate, covered, for about 1 hour, until firm.

2. Meanwhile, prepare the lemon curd. In a medium saucepan, whisk together the sugar, water, flour, lemon zest and juice, salt, and eggs. Over medium-low heat, cook for 8–10 minutes, until thickened, stirring frequently. Pour into a chilled bowl and cool, stirring occasionally to keep a skin from forming. Refrigerate until very cold and thickened.

3. Preheat the oven to 350°F. Using a teaspoon, scoop out the dough and form into thirty-six ¾-inch balls. Press a ball of dough onto the bottom and sides of tiny petit four, fluted tart, or brioche molds. Prick the bottom and sides of the dough to prevent puffing. Place the molds on baking sheets and bake for about 15 minutes, until just golden. Remove the molds to a wire rack to cool for 10 minutes, then carefully remove the cookie-tart shells from the molds to cool completely on wire racks.

4. Not more than 1 hour before serving, spoon a little lemon curd into each cookie tart. Store unfilled cookies in airtight containers, with waxed paper between the layers.

Cats' Tongues

These delicate French cookies are shaped like a cat's tongue. Serve with fruit desserts or ice cream. **Makes about 4 dozen small cookies**

Butter, for greasing
⅔ cup butter, softened
2 cups confectioners' sugar
1 teaspoon vanilla extract
5 egg whites
2 cups all-purpose flour, sifted

1. Preheat the oven to 400°F. Generously butter two large baking sheets. In a medium bowl, using an electric mixer, beat the butter until creamy. Gradually beat in the confectioners' sugar until light and fluffy, then beat in the vanilla extract. Add the egg whites gradually, alternating with the sifted flour, folding in until a firm dough forms.

2. Spoon the dough into a large pastry bag fitted with a plain tip. Pipe strips of dough, 1½–2 inches long, about 2 inches apart onto the baking sheets (the cookies will spread during baking).

3. Bake for 10–12 minutes, until the edges of the cookies are brown and the centers still light. Remove the baking sheets to wire racks to cool slightly. Using a thin-bladed metal spatula, remove the cookies to wire racks to cool completely and become crisp. Store in airtight containers.

Florentines

Florentines are an Italian-style cookie, made from a batter-type dough. They are filled with candied peel and coated with chocolate on one side. **Makes about 30 cookies**

Vegetable oil spray
or vegetable oil,
for greasing

½ cup heavy cream
¼ cup (½ stick)
butter
½ cup superfine sugar
2 tablespoons honey
1⅔ cups slivered
almonds
5 tablespoons
all-purpose flour
Grated zest of 1 orange

¾ teaspoon ground
cinnamon
½ cup diced candied
orange peel
½ cup diced candied
citron (lemon peel)
½ cup diced candied
cherries
8 oz. semisweet
chocolate, melted

1. Preheat the oven to 350°F. Lightly spray or grease two large, nonstick baking sheets. In a medium saucepan over low heat, stir the heavy cream, butter, superfine sugar, and honey until the sugar is dissolved. Increase the heat to high and bring the mixture to a boil, stirring constantly. Remove the pan from the heat and stir in the almonds, flour, orange zest, and

ground cinnamon until well blended, then stir in the diced candied fruits.

2. Drop the mixture by teaspoonfuls, at least 3 inches apart, onto the baking sheets. Using the back of a moistened spoon, carefully spread each circle as thinly as possible.

3. Bake for 8–10 minutes, until the edges are golden and the cookies are bubbling. Do not overbake, since the cookies can burn easily, but do not underbake or the cookies will be too sticky to handle. Remove the baking

sheets to wire racks to cool slightly. For perfectly round cookies, use a 3-inch round cookie cutter to cut around the edges while the cookies are still hot on the baking sheet. Cool slightly until just set. Using a thin-bladed metal spatula, remove the cookies to wire racks to cool completely.

4. When completely cooled, spread the cookies with the melted chocolate on the flat side of each cookie and place, chocolate side up, on wire racks. Refrigerate for

2–3 minutes, until the chocolate is just setting. If you like, using a serrated knife or four-tined fork, make wavy lines on the chocolate layer. Refrigerate for 10–15 minutes to set completely. Store in the refrigerator in airtight containers, with waxed paper between the layers.

RIGHT: *With its cheeky grin and quirky dress sense, the Squirrel is a lovely example of "brush" jars.*

Hazelnut Florentines

These delicious Florentines contain hazelnuts rather than the more usual combination of almonds and candied fruit.

Makes about 2 dozen cookies

1 lb. shelled
  hazelnuts
Vegetable oil spray
  or vegetable oil,
  for greasing
1 cup sugar
½ cup honey
½ cup heavy cream
1 cup (2 sticks) butter

6 oz. white chocolate,
  melted
6 oz. semisweet
  chocolate, melted

RIGHT: *This
promotional jar is
instantly recognizable
as an Oreo cookie.*

1. Preheat the oven to 375°F. Spread the hazelnuts on a baking sheet and bake for 10–12 minutes, stirring once or twice. Pour onto a dry dishcloth and rub together to loosen the skins. Pour into a colander and separate the skins from the nuts. Set aside.

2. Lightly spray or grease two large baking sheets. Place the cooled hazelnuts in a plastic bag, tie securely, and roll the nuts with a rolling pin to crush roughly.

2. In a large, heavy-based saucepan over low heat, stir the sugar, honey, cream, and butter until the sugar is dissolved. Bring to a boil, stirring constantly, and cook rapidly for about 1½ minutes. Remove from the heat and stir in the nuts.

3. Drop teaspoonfuls of the mixture, 3 inches apart, onto the baking sheets. Spread each circle using the back of a moistened spoon. Bake for 8–10 minutes, until the edges are

golden. Remove baking sheets to wire racks to cool slightly. When the cookies are almost set, remove with a thin-bladed metal spatula and place on wire racks to cool completely.
4. Spread the melted white chocolate on one half of each cookie and the melted semisweet chocolate on the other half. Allow the chocolate to cool slightly, then use a fork to make a pattern in the chocolate. Allow to set completely. Store in airtight containers, with waxed paper between the layers.

CLOCKWISE FROM RIGHT: *Lemon Pizzelles, Coconut Fortune Cookies, and Fried Bow Ties*

Coconut Fortune Cookies

These Chinese-style fortune cookies are so much fun to make—and delicious, too! They make a great simple dessert after an Asian-style meal. **Makes about 4 dozen cookies**

Vegetable oil, for greasing

All-purpose flour

2 egg whites

1/3 cup confectioners' sugar, sifted

1 teaspoon coconut or almond extract

2 tablespoons unsalted butter, melted

1/3 cup cake flour, sifted

1/4 cup sweetened shredded coconut, toasted and chopped

1. Grease and flour two large baking sheets (or more if you have them). Using a 3-inch round cookie cutter, glass, or ramekin, mark two circles in diagonal corners of each sheet (the cookies will spread).

2. In a medium bowl, using an electric mixer, beat the egg whites until foamy. Gradually beat in the confectioners' sugar, coconut or almond extract, and melted butter. On low speed, beat in the flour until well blended and smooth.

3. Heat the oven to 350°F. Drop a level teaspoon of batter in the center of each marked circle on the baking sheets. Using the back of a moistened spoon, spread the batter evenly to cover the circles completely. Sprinkle each circle with toasted coconut.

4. Bake, one sheet at a time, for 5 minutes, until the cookie edges are lightly browned. Remove the baking sheet to a wire rack and use a thin-bladed metal spatula to loosen the cookies. Set on a board, fold in half, and with

the fold facing up, bend each cookie over the rim of a glass, creating the classic shape. Hold for 30 seconds. Place on a wire rack to cool.
5. Repeat with the remaining cookies. If the cookies become too crisp to shape, return to the oven for 30 seconds. Repeat with the remaining batter. Store in airtight containers, with waxed paper between the layers.

RIGHT: *A Starnes Rag Doll, produced during the 1940s and 1950s, is a great cookie jar for kids.*

Fried Bow Ties

Traditional in many countries such as Mexico, Italy, Spain, and the Middle East, these cookies are fried, not baked. **Makes about 6 dozen cookies**

3 eggs
¼ cup milk
¼ cup sugar
½ teaspoon salt

2 teaspoons vanilla
*   extract*
2¾ cups all-purpose
*   flour*
Vegetable oil, for frying
Confectioners' sugar,
*   for dusting*

1. In a large bowl, using an electric mixer, beat the eggs, milk, sugar, salt, and vanilla extract until blended. On low speed, beat in 1½ cups of the flour, then stir in the remaining flour to form a soft dough. Scrape the dough onto a sheet of plastic wrap or waxed paper and flatten to a disk shape. Refrigerate for 2–3 hours, until firm.

2. On a lightly floured surface, using a floured rolling pin, roll out half the dough, as thinly as possible, ⅛ inch thick or thinner.

Cut the dough into 4 x 1½-inch strips. With a sharp knife, cut a 1-inch lengthwise slit in the center of each strip. Carefully pull one end of the rectangle through the center slit, and pull through to form the bow tie shape. Continue with the remaining dough.

3. In a deep-fat fryer or deep-sided, heavy frying pan, heat about 2 inches of oil to

Good Things to Eat

MADE WITH
ARM & HAMMER BAKING SODA
77TH EDITION

350°F using a deep-fat thermometer. Carefully drop in a few bow ties at a time and fry for about 1½ minutes, until golden. With a slotted metal spatula or spoon, remove the bow ties to a double thickness of paper towels to drain. Cool completely, then dust with confectioners' sugar. The bow ties are best when eaten the same day.

Lemon Pizzelles

Makes about 3 dozen wedges

1 ¾ cups all-purpose
   flour
2 teaspoons baking
   powder
½ teaspoon salt
3 eggs, lightly beaten
¾ cup sugar
½ cup (1 stick)
   unsalted
   butter, melted

Grated zest of 1 lemon
1 tablespoon lemon
   extract
Confectioners' sugar,
   for dusting

1. Preheat a 7-inch electric pizzelle or waffle iron as the manufacturer directs. Sift the flour, baking powder, and salt into a large bowl.

2. Make a well in the center of the flour mixture and pour in the eggs, sugar, melted butter, lemon zest, and lemon extract. Using an electric mixer on low speed, beat the liquid ingredients until blended, then slowly incorporate the flour from the edge of the well until all the mixture is smooth. Thin with a little milk or water if necessary.

3. Using a small ladle, pour 2 tablespoons of batter into the center of the pizzelle or waffle iron. Pull down the cover and allow to bake, without lifting the cover, for the time specified by the manufacturer.

4. Lift the cover and use a thin-bladed metal spatula or fork to lift the edge of the cookie. Slide the cookies onto a wire rack to cool completely. Repeat with the remaining batter. Dust the cookies with confectioners' sugar and store in airtight containers. Alternatively, keep the pizzelles warm in an oven heated to 250°F while baking, and serve the cookies warm, dusted with confectioners' sugar and topped with a little of your favorite preserves or maple syrup and ice cream.

French Almond Tile Cookies

These popular French cookies—tuiles aux amandes—are so called because they resemble the curved roof tiles seen all over France. **Makes about 2½ dozen cookies**

½ cup whole, blanched
  almonds, lightly toasted
½ cup superfine sugar
Butter, for greasing
3 tablespoons
  unsalted butter,
  softened
2 egg whites
½ teaspoon almond
  extract

¼ cup cake flour,
  sifted
¼ cup flaked almonds

1. Put the blanched almonds and 2 tablespoons of the sugar in the bowl of a food processor. Using the metal blade, process until fine crumbs form. Pour into a small bowl and set aside.

2. Preheat the oven to 400°F. Generously butter two baking sheets (or more if you have them). In a medium bowl, using an electric mixer, beat the butter for about 1 minute, until creamy. Add the remaining sugar and beat for about 1 minute, until light and fluffy.

 *Special Cookies*

Gradually beat in the egg whites and almond extract until blended. Sift over the already-sifted flour and fold into the butter mixture, then fold in the almond-sugar mixture.

3. Begin by working in batches of four cookies on each sheet. Drop tablespoonfuls of batter about 6 inches apart onto a baking sheet. Using the back of a moistened spoon, spread each mound of batter into very thin 3-inch rounds. Each round should be transparent. It does not matter if you make a few holes—the batter will spread evenly and fill them in. Sprinkle the tops with some flaked almonds.

4. Bake, one sheet at a time, for 4–5 minutes, until the cookie edges are lightly browned and the centers are just golden. Remove the baking sheet to a wire rack and, working quickly, use a thin-bladed metal spatula to loosen the edge of a hot cookie. Transfer to a rolling pin and gently press the sides down. Repeat with the remaining cookie rounds.

5. If the cookies become too firm to transfer from the baking sheet, return the sheet to the oven for 30 seconds to soften the cookie dough, then proceed as above. Continue baking and shaping with the remaining dough. When cool, transfer the cookies immediately to airtight containers in single layers. These cookies are very fragile.

RIGHT: *The Dutch Girl, made by the Red Wing Pottery Company of Minnesota.*

Cranberry-Filled Hearts

The cranberry-raspberry filling in these hearts looks stunning and provides a contrast to the sweet, rich cookie dough. **Makes about 20 cookies**

2 1/4 cups all-purpose
  flour
1 1/2 teaspoons baking
  powder
1/2 teaspoon ground
  cinnamon
1/4 teaspoon salt
3/4 cup (1 1/2 sticks)
  unsalted butter,
  softened
1/2 cup sugar

1/4 cup packed light
  brown sugar
1 egg, lightly beaten
2 teaspoons vanilla
  extract
Grated zest of 1 lemon

FILLING

1 cup fresh or frozen
  (defrosted) cranberries
3 tablespoons sugar

3/4 cup raspberry
  preserves
1 tablespoon lemon juice
Confectioners' sugar,
  for dusting

1. Sift the flour, baking powder, cinnamon, and salt into a bowl and set aside. In a large bowl, using an electric mixer, beat the butter and sugars for about 2 minutes, until light and fluffy. Beat in the egg, vanilla extract, and lemon zest until well blended. Stir in the flour mixture until a soft dough forms.

2. Scrape the dough onto a piece of plastic wrap or waxed paper. Using the wrap or paper as a guide, shape the dough into a flat disk and refrigerate for 1–2 hours, until firm enough to roll. The dough can be prepared up to two days ahead.

3. Preheat the oven to 350°F. Lightly grease two large, nonstick baking sheets. On a lightly floured surface, using a floured rolling pin, roll out one third of the dough ⅛ inch thick. (Keep remaining dough refrigerated.) Using a 3½-inch heart-shaped cutter, cut out as many hearts as possible. Using a 1½- or 2-inch heart-shaped cutter, cut out the center of half the heart-shaped cookies. Arrange the cookies on baking sheets, ½ inch apart. Refrigerate the cookies for 15 minutes.

4. Bake the cookies for about 8 minutes, until just set and the edges are golden. Remove the baking sheets to wire racks and, using a metal spatula, transfer the cookies to wire racks to cool completely. Repeat with the remaining dough and all the trimmings.

5. In a food processor with a metal blade attached, process the cranberries, sugar, preserves, and lemon juice. Scrape into a saucepan and cook over medium heat for about 8 minutes, until reduced to about 1 cup, stirring often. Set aside to cool.

6. Spread each whole cookie heart with about 1 tablespoon cranberry mixture to within ½ inch of the edge. Generously dust the cut-out hearts with confectioners' sugar, place over the filling, and press together. Allow the cookies to set for 1 hour at room temperature. Store in airtight containers, with waxed paper between layers.

Ladyfingers

This is a traditional French cookie. Although the piping takes practice to achieve even shapes, the batter is quick and easy to prepare. These elegant cookies can be used to line charlotte molds or make tiramisu. **Makes about 3 dozen**

4 eggs, separated
¾ cup superfine sugar
1 teaspoon vanilla
  extract
¾ cup all-purpose flour,
  sifted twice
⅛ teaspoon cream of
  tartar
Confectioners' sugar,
  for dusting

1. Preheat the oven to 350°F. Lightly grease and flour two large baking sheets. In a medium bowl, using an electric mixer, beat the egg yolks, ½ cup sugar, and vanilla extract for 10 minutes, until thick and sticky and the mixture leaves a ribbon trail when the beaters are lifted from the bowl. Gently fold in the flour until just blended. Do not overbeat.

2. In a large bowl, using clean beaters, beat the egg whites and cream of tartar on low speed until foamy. Increase speed and continue beating until stiff peaks form. Sprinkle in the remaining sugar, a tablespoon at a time, beating well after each addition, until stiff and glossy. Fold a third of the egg whites into the yolk mixture, then, in three batches, fold the yolk mixture into the remaining whites.

3. Gently spoon the batter into a large pastry bag fitted with a ½-inch plain tip. Pipe the batter in 3½-inch lengths, 1½ inches apart, onto the prepared baking sheets. Dust the cookies generously with confectioners' sugar.

4. Bake for about 12 minutes, until golden. Remove the baking sheets to wire racks to cool for 5–7 minutes. Using a metal palette knife or spatula, remove the ladyfingers to wire racks to cool completely. If you like, dust again with confectioners' sugar. Store in an airtight container.

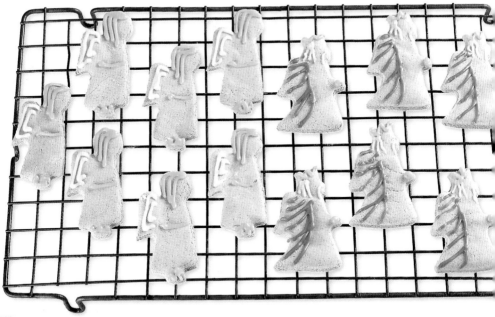

Springerle

These German cookies are traditionally made with a special springerle mold or embossed rolling pin. They are very hard cookies, meant to be stored for long periods in the winter. **Makes about 6 dozen cookies**

4 eggs

2 cups sugar

1 1/2 teaspoons anise extract

4–4 1/2 cups all-purpose flour

1 cup confectioners' sugar

Food coloring

1. In a large bowl, using an electric mixer, beat the eggs and sugar for about 10 minutes, until very thick and sticky and the mixture leaves a ribbon trail when the beaters are lifted from the bowl. On low speed, beat in the anise extract and 4 cups of flour until a firm dough forms; you may need to add a little more flour.

2. Scrape the dough onto a piece of plastic wrap or waxed paper and, using the wrap or

paper, form into a flat disk shape. Wrap tightly and refrigerate for 1 hour (any longer, and the dough may be too firm to roll).

3. On a lightly floured surface, roll out half the dough into a rectangle about ¼ inch thick (the width of the rectangle should be the same width as the embossed rolling pin or multiples of the springerle mold). Lightly flour the springerle rolling pin or mold and tap off any excess flour. Roll or press firmly over the dough, pressing as firmly as possible to obtain a clear imprint in the dough. (If you do not have a springerle mold or embossed rolling pin, you can simply use an appropriately shaped cookie cutter.)

4. Using a sharp knife or pastry wheel, cut the dough between each pattern and place the cookies ½ inch apart on two large, nonstick baking sheets. Repeat with the remaining dough and trimmings. Allow the cookies to stand uncovered at room temperature overnight to dry out.

5. Preheat the oven to 300°F. Bake for about 25 minutes, until the cookies are very slightly browned, rotating baking sheets between the top and bottom shelves, and from front to back, halfway through the cooking time. They should be cooked through but not overbaked, or they will be too hard. Using a spatula, transfer to wire racks to cool completely.

6. To decorate, mix the confectioners' sugar with a little water until a piping consistency is achieved. Add a favorite food color and pipe the icing onto the raised design. Allow to dry completely before storing in airtight containers to "ripen" for a few weeks.

TIP

○ **To use the cookies as tree decorations, make a small hole in the top of each cookie before baking, then thread a pretty ribbon through the baked cookie and tie onto the tree.**

Palmiers

Originating in France, these unusual and attractive cookies are surprisingly simple to make. **Makes 10–12 cookies**

*Vegetable oil spray
or vegetable oil,
for greasing
8 oz. fresh or frozen
puff pastry (defrosted
if frozen)
3 tablespoons sugar
Confectioners' sugar,
for dusting*

1. Preheat the oven to 400°F. Lightly spray or grease a large baking sheet. Roll out the pastry to form about a 10 x 6-inch rectangle. Sprinkle a work surface with half the sugar. Place the dough on the sugared surface and sprinkle with the remaining sugar. Roll the rolling pin lightly over the dough to make the sugar stick.

2. Roll each long side of the dough up to the middle to meet. For easy slicing, place the rolled dough in the freezer for 20 minutes.

Slice the rolled dough into ½-inch slices and arrange 2 inches apart on the baking sheet. Bake for 20 minutes, until golden brown.
3. Remove the baking sheet to a wire rack to cool slightly. Using a thin-bladed metal spatula, remove the cookies to a wire rack to cool completely. Sprinkle with confectioners' sugar. Store in an airtight container.

LEFT: *Cross-eyed from eating too many cookies? The Little Tiger jar was made by California Originals.*

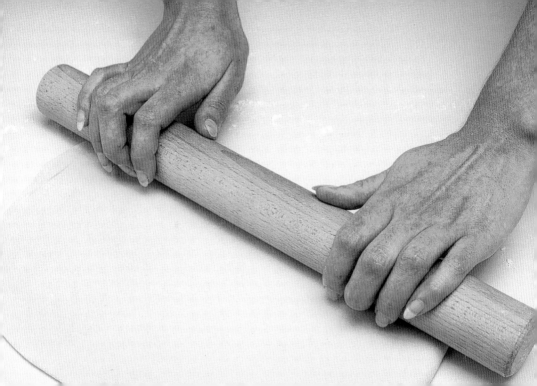

Health-Conscious

recipes

Sunflower Carob Cookies

*A combination of wheat, oats, bran, and sunflower seeds results in a chewy,
satisfying cookie that gives a great midmorning energy boost.*

Makes about 2 dozen cookies

Vegetable oil spray
  or vegetable oil,
  for greasing
1/2 cup (1 stick)
  margarine, softened
1/2 cup light brown sugar
1 egg, beaten
1 teaspoon vanilla
  extract

1/2 teaspoon baking soda
1/2 teaspoon salt
1/2 cup bran
1 cup old-fashioned
  rolled oats
1 cup whole-wheat flour,
  sifted
2 oz. sunflower seeds
4 oz. carob drops

1. Preheat the oven to 375°F. Lightly spray or grease two large baking sheets. In a medium bowl, using an electric mixer, beat the margarine and sugar until light and fluffy. Gradually beat in the egg and vanilla extract until well blended.

2. Add the baking soda, salt, bran, oats, and sifted flour and beat until well blended and a stiff dough forms. Stir in the sunflower seeds and carob drops.

3. Drop heaping tablespoonfuls of the mixture 3 inches apart onto the baking sheets and flatten slightly. Bake 8–10 minutes, until crisp and golden. Remove the baking sheets to wire racks to cool slightly, then transfer the cookies to wire racks to cool completely. Store in airtight containers.

FAR RIGHT: *The Mouse Chef jar, made by the Metlox Company of Manhattan Beach, California.*

Lebkuchen

Although this famous Austrian cookie contains no fat, it has a lovely, cakelike texture. **Makes about 3 dozen cookies**

2 cups all-purpose flour
½ cup rye flour
2 teaspoons baking powder
1 ½ teaspoons ground cinnamon
1 teaspoon ground nutmeg
1 teaspoon ground cloves
1 teaspoon allspice
½ teaspoon salt

½ teaspoon finely ground black pepper
1 egg, lightly beaten
1 cup honey
¾ cup packed light or dark brown sugar
Grated zest of 1 lemon
1 tablespoon fresh lemon juice
1 cup chopped almonds

1 cup diced candied citron (lemon peel)

GLAZE

1 ½ cups confectioners' sugar, sifted
4 teaspoons lemon juice
3 teaspoons water

1. Preheat the oven to 350°F. Lightly grease two large baking sheets. In a large bowl, combine the flours, baking powder, ground cinnamon, nutmeg, cloves, allspice, salt, and pepper. Remove 1 cup of the flour mixture and set aside. Make a well in the center of the remaining flour mixture and add the egg, honey, sugar, lemon zest, and juice.

2. With an electric mixer at low speed, and beginning in the well, beat the ingredients until blended. Add the almonds, candied citron, and enough of the remaining flour to form a stiff dough.

3. Drop heaping tablespoonfuls of the dough, 2 inches apart, onto the prepared baking sheet. Bake for 20 minutes or until a toothpick inserted in the center comes out clean. Remove cookies to wire racks to cool. Repeat with the remaining cookie dough.

4. In a small bowl, mix the confectioners' sugar, lemon juice, and water to form a glaze. Arrange the cookies on a wire rack over a baking sheet (to catch drips) and pour or drizzle a little glaze over each cookie (the glaze may crack as it dries). Store the cookies in an airtight container.

TIP

○ **To soften honey, set the jar in a small saucepan of hot water for 5–10 minutes or microwave on high at 10-second intervals until soft.**

Carob Truffle Squares

This no-bake recipe uses carob, a useful alternative to chocolate that has a similar texture without any of the caffeine. **Makes about 16 squares**

2 cups graham crackers, broken up

½ cup (1 stick) margarine

1 tablespoon light brown sugar

3 tablespoons carob powder

2 tablespoons corn syrup

1 cup raisins

8-oz. carob bar, chopped

1. Place the graham crackers in a plastic freezer bag and crush finely with a rolling pin. Transfer to a large mixing bowl.

2. In a medium saucepan over low heat, heat the margarine, sugar, carob powder, and corn syrup until melted and smooth, stirring continuously. Stir into the cracker crumbs, add the raisins, and stir until well blended. Spread the mixture into an 8-inch square nonstick baking pan, smoothing the top.

3. Put the chopped carob into a heatproof bowl and place over a pan of simmering water, stirring until melted. Using a thin-bladed metal spatula, spread melted carob over the crumb base. Draw the prongs of a fork across the top to make a lined pattern.

4. Refrigerate for 2–4 hours or until chilled, then cut into squares and store in an airtight container.

Seed and Oat Cookies

Seeds are an excellent source of minerals and add a delicious flavor to these little cookies.

Makes about 20 small cookies

Vegetable oil spray
  or vegetable oil,
  for greasing
2 cups old-fashioned
  rolled oats
2 cups all-purpose flour,
  sifted
1 1/2 cups sunflower seeds
4 tablespoons sesame
  seeds

1 teaspoon allspice
1 cup (2 sticks)
  margarine
2 tablespoons soft
  brown sugar
2 teaspoons molasses
1 teaspoon baking soda
2 tablespoons boiling
  water
1 1/2 cups carob drops

Great natural "go-togethers"—Sunshine Hydrox Cookies with milk, coffee... ice cream and other desserts! For downright good eating, you can't beat Hydrox. It's the original cream-filled chocolate cookie. Finest ever made!

1. Preheat the oven to 375°F. Lightly spray or grease two large baking sheets. In a large bowl, combine the oats, sifted flour, sunflower seeds, sesame seeds, and allspice.

2. In a medium saucepan over low heat, heat the margarine, sugar, and molasses until melted and smooth, stirring occasionally. Remove from heat, add the baking soda and water, and stir well. Pour into the oat mixture and stir until blended.

3. Drop heaping teaspoonfuls of the mixture onto the baking sheets at least 2 inches apart.

Bake for about 10 minutes, until golden and set. Remove the baking sheets to wire racks and allow to cool completely. Transfer the cookies to wire racks.

4. Melt the carob drops in a bowl set over just simmering water and place teaspoonfuls of the melted carob over the cookies. Allow to set. Store in an airtight container.

RIGHT: *Who would dare lift the lid of this Tasmanian Devil jar to steal a cookie?*

Pear and Cherry Bars

Dried cherries and pear puree give these moist bars a pleasant, fruity flavor. They're relatively low in fat, too. **Makes about 12 bars**

1 cup less 1 tablespoon
  all-purpose flour
1 tablespoon cocoa
  powder
½ teaspoon ground
  cinnamon
½ teaspoon baking
  soda
¼ teaspoon salt
2 tablespoons sunflower
  margarine

2 large pears
2 teaspoons lemon juice
1 egg, beaten
2 tablespoons sugar
½ cup dried sour
  cherries
1 tablespoon pear juice
  concentrate, to glaze

LEFT: *Raisin and Apricot Bars and Pear and Cherry Bars*

1. Preheat the oven to 350°F. Sift the flour with the cocoa powder, cinnamon, baking soda, and salt in a bowl. Using a pastry blender or your fingers, cut in the margarine.

TIP

○ **Pear juice concentrate is available in health-food stores. Alternatively, mix ¹/₂ cup confectioners' sugar and a little lemon juice for a spreadable glaze.**

2. Peel, quarter, and core the pears. Finely chop the flesh and transfer to a medium bowl. Beat in the lemon juice, beaten egg, and sugar.

3. Stir in the flour mixture until a dough forms, then add the cherries and stir to blend. Spread the mixture into an 8-inch square nonstick baking pan and smooth the top evenly.

4. Bake for 20–25 minutes, until firm. Remove to a wire rack to cool for a few

minutes, then turn out onto the
wire rack. Spread the pear juice
concentrate over the top and leave
to cool before cutting into bars.

RIGHT: *The Metlox Cow with Butterfly is a
particularly pretty jar. Many collectors specialize
in just one type of jar, and Metlox is a popular
brand with collectors.*

Raisin and Apricot Bars

These delicious fruit bars use a dried fruit puree in place of butter to reduce the fat content dramatically. Dried fruit puree also contributes additional nutrients such as dietary fiber, iron, and vitamin A. **Makes about 16 bars**

Vegetable oil spray or oil, for greasing
2 cups dried apricots, soaked overnight
1 tablespoon sunflower or other light vegetable oil

1 cup raisins
1 cup old-fashioned rolled oats
Grated rind of 1 lemon
½ teaspoon cardamom seeds, lightly crushed

1. Preheat the oven to 400°F. Spray or oil a 13 x 9-inch nonstick baking pan. Drain the apricots, reserving the soaking water. Place the apricots in a small saucepan with enough of the soaking water to cover them, and simmer over medium heat for about 5 minutes.

2. Drain off any excess liquid from the apricots and mash them in a large bowl using a potato masher (or blend to a puree in a food processor). Beat in the oil and set aside to cool.

3. In another bowl, combine the raisins, oats, lemon rind, and cardamom seeds. Add the apricot puree and stir until well blended. Spread the mixture into the baking pan, smoothing the top evenly.

4. Bake for 40–45 minutes, until firm. Remove to a wire rack to cool slightly, then turn out onto a wire rack to cool completely. Cut into bars and store in an airtight container.

Carob-Oat Bars

A good option for a child's party or lunch box, these bars substitute carob for chocolate and are packed with energy-giving ingredients. **Makes about 1 dozen bars**

*Vegetable oil spray
or oil, for greasing
4-oz. carob bar
1/2 cup (1 stick)
margarine
1 tablespoon maple
syrup*

*2 cups old-fashioned
rolled oats
1 cup pitted chopped
dates
1/2 cup unsweetened
shredded coconut*

1. Preheat the oven to 350°F. Invert an 8-inch square baking pan and mold a sheet of foil over the bottom. Remove the foil, turn the pan right-side up, and press the foil into the pan. Lightly spray or grease the foil.

2. Break the carob into a medium saucepan and add the margarine and honey. Set over a very low heat and heat until melted and smooth, stirring frequently. Remove the pan from the heat and stir in the oats, dates, and shredded coconut until well blended.

3. Spoon the mixture into the baking pan and spread evenly, smoothing the top with the back of a spoon. Bake for 25–30 minutes, until the top is lightly browned and crisp.
4. Remove the pan to a wire rack to cool slightly, then mark into bars. Using the foil as a guide, remove from the pan and cut into bars. Store in an airtight container.

RIGHT: *McCoy's Monk jar is cleverly designed to discourage any naughty cookie thieves.*

Peanut Butter Bran Cookies

The use of whole-wheat flour and bran adds valuable fiber to these cookies. **Makes about 2 dozen cookies**

Vegetable oil spray
  or vegetable oil,
  for greasing
¹/₂ cup (1 stick)
  margarine
¹/₂ cup packed dark
  brown sugar
1 egg, beaten
¹/₂ teaspoon vanilla
  extract

1 cup crunchy peanut
  butter
1 cup whole-wheat flour
¹/₂ teaspoon baking
  powder
Pinch of salt
1 cup bran

TO THE FEW WHO ARE NOT OUR CUSTOMERS

Continuing to use the same flour you now have prevents obtaining all that is possible in baking.

And it will be so until you make a change.

Until you buy GOLD MEDAL FLOUR, we cannot help you.

GOLD MEDAL FLOUR helped our customers make twenty-seven hundred million loaves last year — every loaf beautiful, creamy white with a golden bloom on the crust.

Make a change and use Gold Medal Flour — because it will bring results and results are what you want and we want.

WASHBURN–CROSBY CO'S
GOLD MEDAL FLOUR

Right: *With his tray of cookies, this chef jar looks ready to serve.*

1. Preheat the oven to 375°F. Lightly spray or grease two large baking sheets. In a large bowl, using an electric mixer, beat the margarine and sugar for 1–2 minutes, until light and fluffy.

2. Gradually beat in the egg, then the vanilla extract, until well blended. Add the peanut butter and beat until well blended. Sift the flour, baking powder, and salt into a bowl, then stir in the bran. Stir the flour mixture into the butter mixture until a stiff dough forms. Using a teaspoon, scoop out the dough and roll into small balls.

3. Place the dough balls at least 2 inches apart on the baking sheets and flatten slightly using the back of a moistened spoon. Bake for 8–10 minutes, until crisp. Remove the baking sheets to wire racks to cool for about 2 minutes, then transfer the cookies to wire racks to cool completely. Store in airtight containers.

For Delicious Cookies
Everybody Likes.

Standard
Sugar Cookies

for recipe see page 33

Molasses Oaties

Molasses adds an extra taste dimension to these fiber-rich little cookies. Packed with whole-wheat flour and oats, they are a good alternative to conventional cookies.

Makes about 20 cookies

Vegetable oil spray
  or vegetable oil,
  for greasing
1/2 cup (1 stick)
  margarine
1/2 cup packed dark
  brown sugar
1 teaspoon molasses
1 teaspoon boiling
  water

1 teaspoon baking
  soda
1 cup whole-wheat
  flour
1/2 teaspoon baking
  powder
1 cup old-fashioned
  rolled oats

1. Preheat the oven to 325°F. Lightly spray or grease two large baking sheets. In a medium saucepan over low heat, heat the margarine, sugar, and molasses until melted and smooth, stirring frequently. Stir in the boiling water and baking soda and remove from the heat.

2. Sift the flour and baking powder into a bowl and stir in the oats. Stir in the margarine mixture until well blended. Drop rounded teaspoonfuls of the mixture onto the baking

sheets, 2 inches apart. Bake for about
20 minutes, until lightly browned.
Remove the cookies to wire racks to
cool. Store in airtight containers.

VARIATION
**Use ¹/₂ cup oats and ¹/₂ cup
unsweetened shredded coconut and
reduce the amount of sugar slightly.**

Muesli Packaways

Be sure to use an unsweetened muesli for these cookies so that they don't become too sweet. **Makes about 3 dozen cookies**

2¼ cups all-purpose flour

2½ teaspoons baking powder

2 teaspoons ground cinnamon

½ teaspoon ground nutmeg

½ teaspoon baking soda

½ teaspoon salt

1 cup sugar

½ cup (1 stick) unsalted butter, softened

¼ cup fresh orange juice

1 egg

1 cup natural unsweetened muesli cereal

½ cup raisins

½ cup chopped dates

½ cup chopped dried apricots

½ cup chopped walnuts

½ cup quick-cooking oats

RIGHT: *Little Red Riding Hood was one of the most popular cookie jars ever made.*

1. Preheat the oven to 350°F. Lightly grease two large baking sheets. In a medium bowl, stir together the flour, baking powder, ground cinnamon and nutmeg, baking soda, and salt.

2. In a large bowl, using an electric mixer, beat the sugar and butter for 1–2 minutes, until light and fluffy. Slowly beat in the orange juice and egg. Stir in the flour mixture until blended, then stir in the muesli, raisins, dates, apricots, chopped nuts, and oats.

3. Drop rounded tablespoonfuls of the mixture at least 2 inches apart onto the baking sheets. Smooth the tops slightly. Bake for about 15 minutes, until the tops are set and lightly browned, rotating baking sheets between the top and bottom shelves, and from front to back, halfway through cooking. Remove the baking sheets to wire racks to cool slightly, then remove the cookies to wire racks to cool completely. Repeat with the remaining dough. Store in airtight containers.

Index

ACKNOWLEDGMENTS
The publishers wish to thank the following collectors,
organizations, and picture libraries for supplying the
photographs (and/or items for photography) that are
featured in the book. Photographs have been credited
by page number:

■ Johnson & Wales
University Culinary
Archives & Museum:
pages 9, 11, 14, 25, 26, 28,
45, 55, 68, 73, 76, 80, 91,
97, 122, 131, 135, 145,
184, 188, 205, 219, 223,
230, 267, 271, 273, 274,
279, 285, 311, 315, 321,
328, 335, 345, 353, 356,
365, 389, 391, 397
■ Gaslight Advertising
Archives, Commack, NY:
pages 11, 21, 38, 81, 147,
154, 165, 199, 211, 226,
252, 262, 300, 325, 377,
378
■ Louise Messina Daking
and Geoff Daking:
pages 35, 41, 49, 53, 65,
69, 72, 77, 79, 84, 87, 103,
106, 109, 115, 123, 127,
138, 143, 153, 163, 169,
171, 172, 177, 183, 189,
201, 204, 209, 214, 217,
222, 225, 235, 241, 256,
259, 261, 275, 283, 291,
295, 296, 309, 327, 333,
339, 343, 351, 364, 371,
379, 383, 387, 390, 395